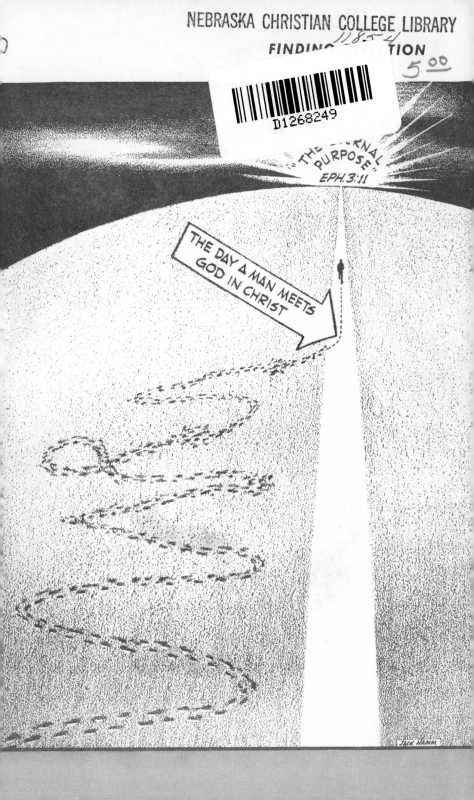

SURVEY COURSE IN CHRISTIAN DOCTRINE

Volume II

BIBLE STUDY TEXTBOOK

SURVEY COURSE IN CHRISTIAN DOCTRINE

Volume II

by

C. C. Crawford, Ph.D. LL.D

College Press, Joplin, Missouri

Copyright 1962

College Press

HUNTER PRINTING
JOPLIN, MISSOURI

CONTENTS

OLD TESTAMENT PREPARATION

NEW TESTAMENT FULFILLMENT

LIST OF ABBREVIATIONS

art., article

cf., compare

ch., chapter

chs., chapters

edit., edition

e.g., for example

ff., following

fn., footnote

ibid., the same

i.e., that is

in loc., in this place
        or connection

intro., introduction

l., line

ll., lines

p., page

pp., pages

par., paragraph

sect., section

sv., under the word

trans., translated

v., verse

vv., verses

vol., volume

Lesson Twenty-Seven
THE PROMISE OF REDEMPTION

Scripture Reading: Gen. 3:9-21.

Scripture to Memorize: "And Jehovah God said unto the serpent, Because thou hast done this, cursed art thou above all cattle, and above every beast of the field; upon thy belly shalt thou go, and dust shalt thou eat all the days of thy life: and I will put enmity between thee and the woman, and between thy seed and her seed: he shall bruise thy head, and thou shalt bruise his heel" (Gen. 3:14-15).

---

1.   Q.   **Do the Scriptures teach that man in his present state is totally depraved?**

     A.   **They teach that he is depraved in consequence of his estrangement from God, but not that he is totally depraved.**

(1) Man in his present unnatural state is alienated from God by sin, and consequently more or less depraved. Eph. 2:3—"among whom we also all once lived in the lusts of our flesh, doing the desires of the flesh and of the mind, and were by nature children of wrath." Col. 1:21—"and you, being in time past alienated and enemies in your mind in your evil works," etc. Paul describes the depravity of heathen nations, in Rom. 1:24-32. Cf. Jude 4, 8, 10-16, 18-19, etc. (2) Man is not totally depraved however, i. e., "wholly defiled in all the faculties and parts of soul and body," as the creeds give it. If man were totally depraved, he would be hopelessly lost; and all the overtures issuing from God's love, all efforts of the Holy Spirit to touch his heart and quicken it to repentance and obedience, and all proclamations of the gospel designed to convict him of sin and of righteousness and judgment, would all be in vain. (3) The devil and his angels are of course totally depraved. But the precise degree of man's spiritual derangement is no-

where clearly indicated in scripture. "But that it is of the positive or comparative and not of the superlative grade, is evident from our own daily observation and experience. Nothing is more common than to see wicked men growing worse and worse under the influence of their own personal transgressions. But if all men were as bad by nature as sin can make them, there could, of course, be no progress in human depravity. . . . The presumptuous sin committed against the Holy Spirit is a personal sin, and it is this, and this only, which fills up a man's cup of iniquity and makes him totally depraved" (Milligan, **Scheme of Redemption,** p. 58). See Matt. 12:31-32.

2. Q.   **In view of man's ability, even in his present fallen state, to respond to the overtures and calls of God, what has God done for him?**

    A.   **God has worked out a Plan of Redemption for him.**

3. Q.   **Why did God work out a Plan of Redemption for man?**

    A.   **God worked out a Plan of Redemption for man because He loves him.**

Because man lapsed into sin and was in danger of perishing in sin for ever, God, out of His great love for him, planned and worked out a plan to avert such a tragedy. John 3:16, 17—"For God so loved the world, that he gave his only begotten Son, that whosoever believeth on him should not perish, but have eternal life. For God sent not the Son into the world to judge the world; but that the world should be saved through him." Rom. 5:8—"But God commendeth his own love toward us, in that, while we were yet sinners, Christ died for us." Eph. 2:4—"but God, being rich in mercy, for his great love wherewith he loved us," etc. 1 John 4:10—"Herein is love, not that we loved God, but that He loved us, and sent His Son to be the propitiation for our sins." Emphasize the fact that if men reject these gifts and calls of God, they will perish forever, in hell, the penitentiary of the moral universe.

4. Q. **When did God first intimate that He proposed to redeem man?**

   A. **He intimated it immediately after the temptation and fall of our first parents.**

Gen. 3:14, 15—"and Jehovah God said unto the serpent . . . I will put enmity between thee and the woman, and between thy seed and her seed; he shall bruise thy head, and thou shalt bruise his heel."

5. Q. **To whom did this mysterious oracle specifically allude?**

   A. **It alluded to Jesus Christ, our Redeemer.**

(1) "In this very mysterious and sublime oracle we have evidently a double reference: 1. To the natural enmity that has ever existed between mankind and the serpent kind; 2. To the warfare that is still carried on between Christ, who is in the highest and most appropriate sense the Seed of the woman, and Satan, who is here symbolically repre-sented by the serpent . . . and here we have, therefore, the first recorded promise of mercy to fallen man. Here began that mighty conflict which is symbolically represented by the enmity that exists between mankind and the serpent kind, but which will not be fully consummated till Christ, the Seed of the woman, shall have completely vanquished Satan and all his host of rebel followers" (Milligan, **Scheme of Redemption**, pp. 64-66). (2) 1 John 3:8—"To this end was the Son of God manifested, that he might destroy the works of the devil." Rom. 16:20—"And the God of peace shall bruise Satan under your feet shortly." See Heb. 2:14-15, Rev. 20:1-3, 7-10.

6. Q. **In what special sense was Jesus the Seed of the woman?**

   A. **In the sense that He was the Seed of a woman ex-clusively, i. e., He had no human father.**

Isa. 7:14—"Therefore the Lord himself will give you a sign: behold, a virgin shall conceive, and bear a son, and shall call his name Immanuel." Matt. 1:20—"Joseph, thou son of David, fear not to take unto thee Mary thy wife; for that which is conceived in her is of the Holy Spirit." Luke 1:35—"The Holy Spirit shall come upon thee, and the power of the Most High shall overshadow thee; wherefore also the holy thing which is begotten shall be called the Son of God." Gal. 4:4—"but when the fulness of the time came, God sent forth his Son, born of a woman, born under the law," etc. Cf. Matt. 1:18-25; Luke 1:26-38; John 1:1-3, 14; 1 Tim. 3:16, etc. Emphasize here the significance of the Virgin Birth. Jesus was the only person who ever came before the world of whom it is claimed that He was the Seed of a woman exclusively.

7. Q. **What would have become of man, if God had not worked out a Plan of Redemption for him?**

A. **He would have been lost forever; because, if God had not provided a sufficient Atonement for the sins of the world, no human being could ever have been saved.**

Without the sufficient Atonement for sin which was provided by Divine grace in the suffering and death of the Lamb of God (John 1:29), there would be for mankind nothing but "a certain fearful expectation of judgment, and a fierceness of fire which shall devour the adversaries" (Heb. 10:27).

8. Q. **Why could no human being ever have been saved, if God had not provided an Atonement for sin?**

A. **Because Divine Justice required an offering adequate to satisfy the Divine government and to sustain the majesty of the Divine law which was violated when man sinned; and no creature, least of all man, was able to provide such an offering.**

This all becomes quite clear when once we realize that sin is transgression of the Divine law, and not of human law. This is an essential truth quite generally overlooked by people of our day and age, who seem to have lost all sense of the true nature of sin and its tragic consequences. Consequently no offering that is of the earth or of earthly origin, no offering that man might bring, could be a sufficient satisfaction for the transgression of Divine law. This is the reason why Cain's offering was rejected: it was an offering of the ground, earthly, and consequently inadequate. See Gen. 4:1-8. In view of man's inability, therefore, to provide an adequate atonement for sin, God provided it for him, i. e., God did for man what man could not do for himself. Otherwise man would have been lost for ever. Cf. Psa. 89:14—"Righteousness and justice are the foundation of thy throne." In view of these sublime truths, our rejection or neglect of God's matchless gifts extended us through Jesus Christ, becomes utterly inexcusable!

REVIEW EXAMINATION OVER LESSON TWENTY-SEVEN

1. Q. Do the Scriptures teach that man in his present state is totally depraved?

2. Q. In view of man's ability, even in his present fallen state, to respond to the overtures and calls of God, what has God done for him?

4. Q. When did God first intimate that He proposed to redeem man?

5. Q. To whom did this mysterious oracle specifically allude?

6. Q. In what special sense was Jesus the Seed of the woman?

7. Q. What would have become of man, if God had not worked out a Plan of Redemption for him?

8. Q. Why could no human being ever have been saved, if God had not provided an Atonement for sin?

Lesson Twenty-Eight
THE ELEMENTS OF TRUE RELIGION

Scripture Reading: Eph. 2:11-22.

Scripture to Memorize: "That he might create in himself of the two one new man, so making peace; and might reconcile them both in one body unto God through the cross" (Eph. 2:15, 16). "But all things are of God, who reconciled us to himself through Christ, and gave unto us the ministry of reconciliation; to wit that God was in Christ reconciling the world unto himself, not reckoning unto them their trespasses, and having committed unto us the word of reconciliation. We are ambassadors therefore on behalf of Christ, as though God were entreating by us: we beseech you on behalf of Christ, be ye reconciled to God" (2 Cor. 5:18-20).

---

9. Q. What was the first necessary step in the unfolding of God's Plan of Redemption for man?

   A. The first necessary step was to reveal the elementary principles, laws and institutions of true religion.

10. Q. What is true religion?

   A. True religion is the system of means of reconciliation whereby man is bound anew to God in covenant relationship.

(1) "Religion, as the term imports, began after the Fall; for it indicates a previous apostasy. A remedial system is for a diseased subject. The primitive man could love, wonder and adore, as angels now do, without religion; but man, fallen and apostate, needs religion in order to his restoration to the love and worship and enjoyment of God. Religion, then, is a system of means of reconciliation—an institution for bringing man back to God—something to bind man anew to love and delight in God" (A. Campbell, Christian Sys-

tem, p. 36). Again: "Religo with all its Latin family, imports a binding again, or tying fast that which was dissolved" (Campbell, **ibid.**, p. 36, fn.). (2) The essential
principle of music is harmony; of art, it is beauty; of government, authority; of sin, selfishness; so the fundamental
principle of true religion is reconciliation. See Eph. 2:11-
22, 2 Cor. 6:18-20.

11. Q. What are the essential elements of true religion?

A. They are: Altar, Sacrifice, and Priesthood.

(Teachers, this truth cannot be impressed too forcefully
upon the minds of your pupils. It underlies all correct
interpretation of the Scriptures, and all correct understanding of God's dealings with the human race.)

12. Q. What are the two departments of true religion?

**A. The two departments of true religion are: (1)
the things that God has done and will do for us;
and (2) the things which we must do for ourselves in obedience to Him; all of which matters,
both on the Divine side and on the human side,
result in binding us anew to Him in covenant
relationship.**

"The whole proposition must of necessity in this case come
from the offended party. Man could propose nothing, do
nothing to propitiate his Creator, after he had rebelled
against Him. Heaven, therefore, overtures; and man ac-
cepts, surrenders and returns to God. The Messiah is a
gift, sacrifice is a gift, justification is a gift, the Holy Spirit
is a gift, eternal life is a gift, and even the means of our
personal sanctification is a gift from God. Truly, we are
saved by grace. Heaven, we say, does certain things for us,
and also proposes to us what we should do to inherit eternal
life . . . We are only asked to accept a sacrifice which God
has provided for our sins, and then the pardon of them,
and to open the doors of our hearts, that the Spirit of God
may come in and make his abode in us. God has provided

all these blessings for us, and only requires us to accept of them freely, without any price or idea of merit on our part. But he asks us to receive them cordially, and to give up our hearts to Him" (Campbell, **ibid.,** p. 36).

13.   Q.   What is the root of true religion on the divine side?

A.   The root of true religion on the divine side is the grace of God.

(1) All the principles, institutions, laws and blessings of true religion issue from the grace of God. "Grace," says Cruden, "is taken for the free and eternal love and favor of God, which is the spring and source of all the benefits which we receive from Him." Dr. Hovey defines grace as "unmerited favor to sinners." (2) The mother who sacrifices herself for her sick child does it, not because she must, but because she loves the child. In like manner, to say that we are saved by grace, is to say that we are saved without necessity on the part of God to save us. This means that God did not provide a Plan of Redemption for man, with its accompanying benefits and blessings, because He was under any kind of obligation to man, or to any other creature, to have done so. It means, rather, that foreseeing man in a lost condition and in grave danger of perishing for ever, God, out of His infinite love for him, arranged, provided and offered the necessary plan and means to reclaim and regenerate him, to build him up in true holiness, and to prepare him for citizenship in heaven. Both creation and redemption have their source and root in God's amazing mercy, love and compassion. Oh, when will the human race become appreciative of this great truth and its far-reaching implications! (3) John 3:16-17. Tit. 2:11—"for the grace of God hath appeared, bringing salvation to all men" (i. e., the promise and offer of salvation). Tit. 3:5—"according to his mercy he saved us." Eph. 2:8—"by grace have ye been saved through faith." Eph. 1:6—"to the praise of

the glory of his grace, which he freely bestowed on us in the Beloved."

14. Q. What is the root of true religion on the human side?

A. The root of true religion on the human side is our faith.

(1) Heb. 11:6—"Without faith it is impossible to be well-pleasing unto him; for he that cometh to God must believe that he is, and that he is a rewarder of them that seek after him." John 14:1—"ye believe in God, believe also in me." Eph. 2:8—"by grace have ye been saved through faith." Rom. 5:1—"being therefore justified by faith, we have peace with God through our Lord Jesus Christ." Gal. 3:26, 27—"For ye are all sons of God, through faith, in Christ Jesus. For as many of you as were baptized into Christ did put on Christ." (2) Every act of a truly religious life issues from our faith. Repentance, for instance, is faith turning the individual from darkness to light and from the power of Satan unto God (Acts 26:18). The good confession is faith declaring itself in the presence of witnesses. Baptism is faith yielding to the authority of Christ. The Lord's Supper is faith remembering Jesus Christ. Prayer is faith communing with God through Christ. Liberality is faith acknowledging God's ownership and man's stewardship. Meditation is faith pondering, and praise is faith exalting our God and His Christ. Faith so motivates the truly religious life, that it is said in scripture that "whatsoever is not of faith is sin" (Rom. 14:23).

15. Q. What is true religion in its practical aspects?

A. It is benevolence and holiness.

Jas. 1:27—"Pure religion and undefiled before our God and Father is this, to visit the fatherless and widows in their affliction, and to keep oneself unspotted from the world."

16. Q. In view of all the Divine arrangements for our redemption, what should we do?

A. The very least we can do, in return for all that
God has done and will do for us, is to love Him
and serve Him faithfully.

God gave His Son for us. The Son gave His life for us.
The Holy Spirit pleads with us, through the gospel, to return to God. To reject all these Divine overtures and calls
and gifts is base ingratitude! Rom. 11:33-36, "O the depth
of the riches both of the wisdom and the knowledge of
God! how unsearchable are his judgments, and his ways
past tracing out! For who hath known the mind of the
Lord? or who hath been his counsellor? or who hath first
given to him, and it shall be recompensed unto him again?
For of him, and through him, and unto him, are all things.
To him be the glory for ever. Amen."

REVIEW EXAMINATION OVER LESSON
TWENTY-EIGHT

9.   Q.   What was the first necessary step in the unfolding of God's Plan of Redemption for man?

10. Q.   What is true religion?

11. Q.   What are the essential elements of true religion?

12. Q.   What are the two departments of true religion?

13. Q.   What is the root of true religion on the divine
side?

14. Q.   What is the root of true religion on the human
side?

15. Q.   What is true religion in its practical aspects?

16. Q.   In view of all the Divine arrangements for our
redemption, what should we do?

Lesson Twenty-Nine
THE BEGINNINGS OF RELIGION

Scripture Reading: Gen. 4:1-16.

Scripture to Memorize: "By faith Abel offered unto God a more excellent sacrifice than Cain, through which he had witness borne to him that he was righteous, God bearing witness in respect of his gifts: and through it he being dead yet speaketh" (Heb. 11:4).

17. Q. What are the two general kinds of religion?
    A. They are: Revealed Religion, and Natural Religion.

18. Q. What do we mean by Revealed Religion?
    A. By Revealed Religion, we mean those systems of religion which God has revealed to man.

19. Q. What do we mean by Natural Religion?
    A. By Natural Religion, we mean the pagan or heathen systems of religion.

20. Q. Why do we speak of the heathen systems of religion as Natural Religion?
    A. Because they are all efforts on the part of mankind to apprehend and know and worship God from the dim light of Nature, as interpreted by the unaided human intelligence.

The religions usually named as pagan or heathen are: Brahmanism, Buddhism, Hinduism, Confucianism, Zoroastrianism, and two or three others akin to these and subordinate. Brahmanism is of India. Buddhism had its origin in India, and spread to China and Japan. Confucianism is of China, as is Taoism. Hinduism is the name given to the multiplicity of cults which prevail in India. Zoroastrianism is derived from Zoroaster, the ancient persian philosopher. Mohammedanism, which originated in the seventh century A. D., is of Arabia; and its founder, Ubul 'l Kassim, later called Mohammed, borrowed his idea of the one God from the revealed religions. Strictly speaking, none of these systems can qualify as a religion, although we popularly speak of them as such. They are in reality ethical, metaphysical or philosophical systems.

21. Q. What is the fundamental difference between these pagan religions and the revealed religions?

A. The fundamental difference is, that all pagan or heathen religions show man seeking after God; whereas in the revealed religions, God is represented as reaching down to reclaim and redeem fallen man.

Job 11:7—"Canst thou by searching find out God? Canst thou find out the Almighty unto perfection?" 1 Cor. 1:21 —"For seeing that in the wisdom of God the world through its wisdom knew not God, it was God's good pleasure through the foolishness of the preaching to save them that believe."

22. Q. What are the inadequacies of all pagan religions?

A. They are inadequate in every respect as spiritual forces.

(1) They lack the authority to retrain the evil passions and propensities of men. (2) They fail to beget and cherish in the human heart a consciousness of sin or a hungering and thirsting after righteousness. (3) They fail to provide an atonement for sin. (4) They fail to offer any plan of salvation from sin. (5) They fail to offer any means of eradicating the consequences of sin, such as physical death, etc. (6) They fail to provide an example of true holiness, such as Jesus gave us in His life. (7) They fail to offer sufficient incentives or means to growth in holiness. (8) In consequence of all these deficiencies, they fail to build a high type of human civilization. They are saturated with such

evils as superstition, animism, asceticism, ancestor worship, sensualism, etc.

23. Q. What are the revealed religions?

A. The revealed religions are: the Patriarchal Religion; the Hebrew or Jewish Religion, commonly called Judaism; and the Christian Religion, commonly called Christianity.

24. Q. Where do we find the authentic record of the principles, laws and institutions of these revealed religions?

A. In the Holy Scriptures.

(1) The laws and institutions of Patriarchal Religion are, recorded in the book of **Genesis.** (2) The Hebrew or Jewish Religion is revealed in the **Old Testament Scriptures.** (3) The Christian Religion is revealed in the **New Testament Scriptures.**

25. Q. What is the only revealed religion that is in force today?

A. The only revealed religion that is in force today is **Christianity.**

Both Patriarchism and Judaism were abrogated and came to an end at the death of Christ. See John 1:17, 2 Cor. 3:1-14, Gal. 3:23-28, Col. 2:13-15, Heb. 8, etc. The only religion through which God promises to enter into covenant relationship with man, in the present Dispensation, is Christianity, the religion revealed aand established by our Lord and Savior Jesus Christ and His Apostles. See John 14:6, 1 Tim. 2:5, Eph. 4:4-6, etc.

26. Q. What was the first institution of revealed religion that God established?

A. The Altar.

27. Q. What was the Altar?

A. The Altar was an artificial erection of earth,

> turf, and unhewn stones, upon which sacrifices
> were offered.

Gen. 8:20—"Noah builded an altar unto Jehovah, and took
of every clean beast, and of every clean bird, and offered
burnt-offerings on the altar." Gen. 12:7, 8—"And Jehovah appeared unto Abram, and said, Unto thy seed will I
give this land; and there builded he an altar unto Jehovah,
who appeared unto him. And he removed from thence
unto the mountain on the east of Bethel, and pitched his
tent, having Bethel on the east, and Ai on the west; and
there he builded an altar unto Jehovah, and called upon
the name of Jehovah." See Gen. 13:18, 22:9, etc. Exo.
20:24-26, "An altar of earth shalt thou make unto me, and
shalt sacrifice thereon thy burnt-offerings, and thy peace-
offerings, thy sheep, and thine oxen; in every place where
I record my name I will come unto thee and I will bless
thee. And if thou make me an altar of stone, thou shalt
not build it of hewn stones; for if thou lift up thy tool
upon it, thou hast polluted it," etc. See Gen. 26:25, 33:20;
Exo. 17:15; Josh. 8:30, 22:10; Judg. 6:25-27, 21:4; 1 Sam.
7:17, 14:35; 2 Sam. 24:21, 25; 1 Ki. 18:30-32; 2 Chron.
4:1, etc.

28. Q. What purpose was the Altar designed to serve?

   A. It was to serve as a place of meeting for man with
      God, who was to be approached with a gift in
      the form of a sacrifice.

29. Q. What was the first positive ordinance of true
       religion that God ordained?

   A. The ordinance of Sacrifice.

30. Q. Where do we find the first mention of Sacrifice
       in the Scriptures?

   A. We find it in connection with the story of Cain
      and Abel, both of whom were sons of Adam and
      Eve.

(1) Gen. 4:3-5, "And in process of time it came to pass, that Cain brought of the fruit of the ground an offering unto Jehovah. And Abel, he also brought of the firstlings of his flock and of the fat thereof. And Jehovah had respect unto Abel and to his offering; but unto Cain and to his offering he had not respect." (2) It is suggested that the story of Cain and Abel be used as the scripture basis for the presentation of this lesson to the smaller children.

31.   Q.   Why did God accept Abel's offering and reject Cain's?

A.   Evidently because Abel's offering conformed to the requirements of God's law of Sacrifice, and Cain's did not.

(1) We are told in Heb. 11:4, that "by faith Abel offered unto God a more excellent sacrifice than Cain, through which he had witness borne to him that he was righteous, God bearing witness in respect of his gifts." The difference, then, was not in their persons, but in their gifts. In Rom. 10:17 we read that faith comes from hearing the Divine word. We therefore conclude that God must have ordained Sacrifice and specified its essential features, as soon no doubt as our first parents lapsed into sin; and that Abel brought an offering which conformed to the law of Sacrifice in every particular, whereas Cain's offering failed to meet the Divine requirements. (2) The acceptance of Abel's offering was, then, in consequence of his faith, which was evidenced by his implicit obedience to God's commands. On the other hand, Cain's offering was rejected because it was not in conformity to the law of Sacrifice, and hence manifested a spirit of presumption and unbelief; the same spirit which, later, led him to commit murder. See Gen. 4:8-16.

32.   Q.   What was the essential difference between Abel's offering and Cain's offering, that resulted in God's acceptance of the former and His rejection of the latter?

A. We conclude that the difference was in the fact that Abel's offering was a blood sacrifice, and Cain's offering was not a blood sacrifice.

(1) Cain presented to Jehovah an offering of the ground. But the ground itself had already been placed under a divine anathema. Gen. 3:17—"Cursed is the ground for thy sake," etc. In short, it is evident that Cain wilfully and presumptuously disobeyed God; hence his offering was rejected. (2) Lev. 17:11—"For the life of the flesh is in the blood; and I have given it to you upon the altar to make atonement for your souls; for it is the blood that maketh atonement by reason of the life." Heb. 9:22—"and according to the law, I may almost say, all things are cleansed with blood, and apart from shedding of blood there is no remission." (3) It will thus be seen that Abel's offering was in strict conformity to the law of Sacrifice in at least three particulars, viz., the victim was a "firstling" of his flock, its life was taken, and its blood was shed. Hence it was by faith that "Abel offered unto God a more excellent sacrifice than Cain."

33. Q. What important lesson, respecting Divine ordinances, should we derive from this incident?

A. We should learn that men have no right to alter the ordinances of God in any particular; that for man to do so is, in fact, to manifest a spirit of presumption and unbelief.

The Divine ordinances are sacred trusts which God has given His children to perpetuate, in the manner in which He ordained them to be kept. Baptism, for instance, was originally an immersion of a penitent believer in water, for the remission of sins. By what authority, then, have churchmen and theologians substituted for immersion, the sprinkling or pouring of a small quantity of water on the candidate's head? The answer is: solely by their own authority, and without any Divine warrant for the substitution whatsoever. The result is misunderstanding, confusion and division. Thus do men make void the word of God with their own puerile opinions and traditions. Such is "the way of Cain" (Jude 11)—the way of presumption, unbelief, and ultimate rejection by the heavenly Father.

REVIEW EXAMINATION OVER LESSON
TWENTY-NINE

17. Q. What are the two general kinds of religion?
18. Q. What do we mean by Revealed Religion?
19. Q. What do we mean by Natural Religion?
20. Q. Why do we speak of the heathen systems of religion as Natural Religion?
21. Q. What is the fundamental difference between these pagan religions and the revealed religions?
22. Q. What are the inadequacies of all pagan religions?
23. Q. What are the revealed religions?
24. Q. Where do we find the authentic record of the principles, laws and institutions of these revealed religions?
25. Q. What is the only revealed religion that is in force today?
26. Q. What was the first institution of revealed religion that God established?
27. Q. What was the Altar?
28. Q. What purpose was the Altar designed to serve?
29. Q. What was the first positive ordinance of true religion that God ordained?
30. Q. Where do we find the first mention of Sacrifice in the Scriptures?
31. Q. Why did God accept Abel's offering and reject Cain's?
32. Q. What was the essential difference between Abel's offering and Cain's offering, that resulted in God's acceptance of the former and His rejection of the latter?

33. Q. What important lesson, respecting Divine ordinances, should we derive from this incident?

Lesson Thirty
THE ORDINANCE OF SACRIFICE

Scripture Reading: Heb. 9:16-28.

Scripture to Memorize: "For the life of the flesh is in the blood; and I have given it to you upon the altar to make atonement for your souls: for it is the blood that maketh atonement by reason of the life" (Lev. 17:11). "And according to the law, I may almost say, all things are cleansed with blood, and apart from shedding of blood there is no remission" (Heb. 9:22).

34. Q. What was the first institution of true religion which God established?

A. The Altar.

35. Q. What was the first ordinance of true religion which God established?

A. The ordinance of Sacrifice.

36. Q. What was the ordinance of Sacrifice?

A. It was the solemn infliction of death upon an innocent and unoffending victim, and the subsequent offering of that victim to God upon the altar.

37. Q. To whom was Sacrifice offered?

A. It was offered to God only.

38. Q. For whom was Sacrifice offered?

A. It was offered for man.

39. Q. By whom was Sacrifice offered?

A. It was offered by a priest, or by someone acting in the capacity of a priest.

40. Q. What was the victim customarily offered as a sacrifice for sin in olden times?

A. It was usually a lamb, a firstling of the flock, without blemish or spot. Hence Christ, our Perfect Sacrifice for sin, is referred to in scripture as the Lamb of God "that taketh away the sin of the world" (John 1:29).

Gen. 4:4—"and Abel, he also brought of the firstlings of his flock." Exo. 12:5—"your lamb shall be without blemish, a male a year old." Cf. John 1:29, 36; 1 Pet. 1:19; 1 Cor. 5:7; Rev. 13:8, etc.

41. Q. What is the fourfold design of Sacrifice?

A. As respects God, it is a propitiation; as respects the sinner, it is a reconciliation; as respects sin, it is an expiation; as respects the saved, it is a redemption.

42. Q. In what sense is Sacrifice a propitiation?

A. It is a propitiation, in the sense that it is designed to satisfy the demands of justice upon the sinner.

God's moral kingdom, like His physical world, is established upon a foundation of divine law. Transgression of this divine law is sin. Consequently, when the divine law is disobeyed, justice requires that something be done about it, in order that the sanctity and majesty of the law may be properly sustained. Even under human government, to allow infraction of the civil law to go unpunished or unpropitiated, is to encourage further violation and rebellion, and to eventually, in effect at least, completely nullify the law itself. A great many human teachers, in their eagerness to emphasize the love of God, completely ignore the fact of His unfailing justice. The Psalmist says: "Righteousness and justice are the foundation of thy throne" (Psa. 89:14). This being true, it follows that God cannot consistently allow transgression of His laws to go unpropitiated and at the same time extend mercy to the transgressor. To do so would be to condone sin, and to undermine the foundations of His government. "The indignity offered His person, authority and government, by the rebellion of man, as also the good of all His creatures, made it impossible for Him, according to justice, eternal right, and His own benevolence, to show mercy without sacrifice. . . In this sense only, God could not be gracious to man in forgiving him without a propitiation, or something that could justify Him both to Himself and all His creatures" (Campbell, **Christian System,** p. 39). See Rom. 3:24-26. In short, God could not be infinitely just and extend mercy to the sinner, without an offering from or for the latter, sufficient to satisfy the demands of perfect Justice with respect to the divine law violated. Propitiation is, in a sense, a legal term.

43. Q. **In what sense is Sacrifice a reconciliation?**

A. **It is reconciliation, in the sense that it is designed to bring the offended party and the offender together, and so to make peace between them.**

The offended party is God, the offender is man. So far as it honors law and justice, then, Sacrifice reconciles God to forgive; and so far as it brings love and mercy to the offender, it overcomes the rebellion in his heart and reconciles him to his offended Sovereign. "God's 'anger is turned away' (not a turbulent passion, not an implacable wrath) but 'that moral sentiment of justice' which demands the punishment of violated law, is pacified or well pleased; and man's hatred and animosity against God is subdued, overcome and destroyed in and by the same sacrifice. Thus, in fact, it is, in reference to both parties, a reconciliation" (Campbell, **ibid.,** p. 40). See Eph. 2:15-16, 2 Cor. 5:18-20.

44. Q. **In what sense is Sacrifice an expiation?**

A. **It is an expiation in the sense that it is designed to actually cleanse and purify the heart of the guilt of sin.**

Sacrifice is designed to do even more than to cover sin—it

is designed to cancel it, to put it away, hence to cleanse and purify the heart and life of sin's guilt and pollution. See Heb. 9:26.

45.   Q.   In what sense is Sacrifice a redemption?

A.   It is a redemption in the sense that it is designed to deliver the offerer from the bondage of sin and to consecrate him anew to the service of God.

See Rom. 3:24; 1 Cor. 6:19-20; Acts 20:28; Gal. 3:13, 4:4-5; Eph. 1:7; Col. 1:14; 1 Tim. 2:5-6; Tit. 2:14; Heb. 9:12, 2:14-15; 1 Pet. 1:18-19; Rev. 5:9, etc.

46.   Q.   What is the meaning of the word Atonement?

A.   It is equivalent to Propitiation.

(1) "The Hebrew term copher, translated in the Greek Old Testament by ilasmos, and in the common English version by atonement or propitiation, signifies a covering. The word copher 'to cover' or 'to make atonement,' denotes the object of sacrifice; and hence Jesus is called the ilasmos, the covering, propitiation or atonement for our sins" (Campbell, **ibid.,** p. 38, fn.). (2) 1 John 2:2—"he is the propitiation for our sins." 1 John 4:10—"God ... loved us, and sent His Son to be the propitiation for our sins." (3) To make atonement, means, then, to satisfy the claims of justice with respect to the divine law which has been violated. Lev. 17:11—"it is the blood that maketh atonement by reason of the life." It is thus obvious that atonement and propitiation are synonymous terms.

47.   Q.   What was the typical design of animal sacrifices in olden times?

A.   They were designed to foreshadow and to point forward to the Supreme Sacrifice of the Lamb of God, the Perfect Atonement for 'the sin of the world' (John 1:29).

(1) This is another incontrovertible evidence of the divine origin of Sacrifice. (2) Rev. 5:9—"Worthy art thou to

take the book, and to open the seals thereof: for thou wast slain, and didst purchase unto God with thy blood men of every tribe, and tongue, and people, and nation, and madest them to be unto our God a kingdom and priests; and they reign upon the earth." 1 Pet. 2:24—"who his own self bare our sins in his body upon the tree, that we having died unto sins, might live unto righteousness; by whose stripes ye were healed." Heb. 9:26—"but now once at the end of the ages hath he been manifested to put away sin by the sacrifice of himself."

48. Q. **What great truth did God establish with respect to His ordinances, in the Altar and in Sacrifice?**

A. **He established the truth that all His positive ordinances are divine appointments.**

(1) All positive ordinances are divine appointments. When you agree, for instance, to meet a friend at a certain time and place, that is an appointment. So God's positive ordinances are appointments where Divine grace and human faith meet in a solemn tryst. (2) In olden times God and man met at the altar of sacrifice. See Gen. 22:1-19, Exo. 20:24-26. (3) Similarly, the Christian ordinances are divine appointments. In the ordinance of Christian baptism, God meets the penitent believer and there confers upon him, through the efficacy of the atoning blood of Christ, the full and free blessing of remission of sins. Hence baptism is said, in scripture, to be the institution in which sins are washed away (Acts 22:16); and is also said to be for salvation (Mark 16:16, 1 Pet. 3:21), for remission of sins (Acts 2:38), and for induction into Christ (Gal. 3:26-27). (4) The Lord's Supper is likewise the divinely-appointed observance in which the children of God under the new covenant meet with their Savior, King, and Elder Brother, Jesus Christ, in solemn religious convocation and communion, on each first day of the week. See Matt. 26:26-29, Luke 22:14-20, Acts 20:7, 1 Cor. 10:16, 1 Cor. 11:23-29, etc. (5)

On the human side, then, the ordinances are essentially manifestations and acts of faith. When the truth is once fully appreciated by Christian people that the Lord's ordinances are not rites, forms or meaningless ceremonies; but solemn, spiritual, heart acts, essentially acts of faith, and solemn meetings with our heavenly Father and with our great Redeemer, then indeed a great spiritual awakening will be engendered throughout the whole of Christendom. The thing most needed in this day and age is a correct evaluation of the divine ordinances in the light of scripture teaching.

REVIEW EXAMINATION OVER LESSON THIRTY

34. Q. What was the first institution of true religion which God established?

35. Q. What was the first ordinance of true religion which God established?

36. Q. What was the ordinance of Sacrifice?

37. Q. To whom was Sacrifice offered?

38. Q. For whom was Sacrifice offered?

39. Q. By whom was Sacrifice offered?

40. Q. What was the victim customarily offered as a sacrifice for sin in olden times?

41. Q. What is the fourfold design of Sacrifice?

42. Q. In what sense is Sacrifice a propitiation?

43. Q. In what sense is Sacrifice a reconciliation?

44. Q. In what sense is Sacrifice an expiation?

45. Q. In what sense is Sacrifice a redemption?

46. Q. What is the meaning of the word Atonement?

47. Q. What was the typical design of animal sacrifices in olden times?

48. Q. What great truth did God establish with respect to His ordinances, in the Altar and in Sacrifice?

Lesson Thirty-One

WHAT GOD DID THROUGH THE PATRIARCHS

Scripture Reading: Heb. 11:1-22.

Scripture to Memorize: "Now faith is assurance of things hoped for, a conviction of things not seen" (Heb. 11:1). "Without faith it is impossible to be well-pleasing unto him; for he that cometh to God must believe that he is, and that he is a rewarder of them that seek after him" (Heb. 11:6). "These all died in faith, not having received the promises, but having seen them and greeted them from afar, and having confessed that they were strangers and pilgrims on the earth. For they that say such things make it manifest that they are seeking after a country of their own. And if indeed they had been mindful of that country from which they went out, they would have had opportunity to return. But now they desire a better country, that is, a heavenly: wherefore God is not ashamed of them, to be called their God: for he hath prepared for them a city" (Heb. 11:13-16).

---

49. Q. **What was the first revealed religion?**

     A. **The Patriarchal Religion.**

50. Q. **What was the Patriarchal Religion?**

     A. **It was the religion which prevailed in earliest times, and which was administered by heads of families, men of great faith in God.**

51. Q. **By what name are these men of faith of the most ancient times, known in the Scriptures?**

     A. **They are known as the Patriarchs.**

Acts 7:8, 9—"and Isaac begat Jacob, and Jacob the twelve patriarchs. And the patriarchs, moved with jealousy against Joseph, sold him into Egypt." Heb. 7:4—"Abraham, the patriarch." Acts 2:29—"the patriarch David." etc.

52. Q. Where do we find the history of the Patriarchal Era?

   A. In the book of Genesis.

53. Q. Who were the Patriarchs?

   A. They were men of the most ancient times, who governed their respective families or descendants by paternal right.

54. Q. What is the common designation for Patriarchal government and religion?

   A. It is commonly known as family government and religion, in that the family was the social unit.

As a matter of fact, the family, and not the individual, has been the primary social unit from the beginning of time. The race began with the first family, of which Adam was the father and head, and Eve the mother. God Himself instituted marriage, the home and the family. See Gen. 2:18-25.

55. Q. What was the Patriarchal form of government?

   A. It was that form of government which prevailed in the most ancient times, in which the father of the family retained and exercised authority over his descendants as long as he lived.

56. Q. What was the Patriarchal form of religion?

   A. It was that form of religion in which the Patriarch or father of the family acted as mediator between God and the members of his household.

57. Q. What three offices were administered by a Patriarch by divine authority?

   A. The offices of prophet, priest and king.

(1) As prophet, the Patriarch received God's revelations and handed them on to his household. (2) As priest, he acted as mediator between God and his family, in all the exercises and ordinances of worship; and offered sacrifices for his own sins and the sins of his household. (3) As king,

he was the ruler of his household, and his will was the absolute law from which there was no appeal. The Patri-arch retained this authority over his descendants as long as he lived, regardless of any new connections they may have formed.

58. Q. Who were the outstanding men of the Patri-archal Era?

A. They were: Adam, Abel, Enoch, Noah, Abra-ham, Isaac, Jacob and Joseph.

(1) Adam, the first man, was the progenitor of the human race. (2) The name of Abel, one of his sons, has gone down in sacred history, in connection with the first re-corded instance of sacrifice, as a man of great faith. Gen. 4:1-8, Heb. 11:4. (3) Enoch, who was in the direct line from Adam to Noah, through Seth, was a man of such great faith and piety that God translated him "that he should not see death." Gen. 5:21-24, Heb. 11:5. (4) Noah is described as "a righteous man, and perfect in his genera-tions" (Gen. 6:9). It was through Noah that God per-petuated the human race and preserved His Plan of Re-demption for man, after sweeping away the iniquitous ante-diluvian world in the Deluge. The name of Noah will al-ways be associated in our thinking with the building of the Ark. Gen. chs. 6-9, Heb. 11:7. (5) Abraham was perhaps the greatest of all the Patriarchs. He was originally a Chal-dean, until God called him out of Ur of the Chaldees and made him the father of the Hebrew people. It was with Abraham and his posterity that God originated and estab-lished the old testament. Gen. chs. 12-25, Heb. 11:8-19. (6) Isaac, the child of promise, was the son of Abraham and Sarah. Gen. chs. 21-27, Heb. 11:20. (7) Jacob was the son of Isaac and Rebekah. His name was later changed to Israel, from which the terms "children of Israel" and "Israelites" were derived. He was the father of the twelve "princes" who became the heads of the twelve tribes. Gen.

chs. 27-49, Heb. 11:21. (8) Joseph, the son of Jacob and Rachel, was sold by his brothers into Egyptian bondage, and was subsequently exalted to the high office of Prime Minister of that great nation. Gen. chs. 37-50, Heb. 11:22. The Hebrew people still look back to Abraham, Isaac and Jacob as their national forbears.

59. Q. What fundamental institution of true religion did God establish through the Patriarchs?

A. The Altar.

60. Q. What fundamental ordinance of true religion did God establish through the Patriarchs?

A. The ordinance of Sacrifice.

61. Q. What first essential principle of true religion did God establish through the Patriarchs?

A. The very first principle of true religion, namely, that apart from the shedding of blood there is no remission of sin (Lev. 17:11, Heb. 9:22).

62. Q. Why did God require that sacrifice for sin should include the shedding of blood?

A. Because life is in the blood; consequently a blood sacrifice is the only fit atonement for sin.

Lev. 17:11—"it is the blood that maketh atonement by reason of the life." Heb. 9:22—"apart from shedding of blood there is no remission."

63. Q. Does this mean that the ancients received actual remission of sins through animal sacrifices?

A. No. It means that their sins were passed over from year to year, until the fulness of time came, in which the Perfect Atonement was made for the sins of the whole world.

(1) The animal sacrifices of the Patriarchal and Jewish dispensations could not and did not take away sins. Heb. 10:1-4, "For the law having a shadow of the good things to come, not the very image of the things, can never with

the same sacrifices year by year, which they offer continually, make perfect them that draw nigh . . . but in those
sacrifices there is a remembrance made of sins year by year.
For it is impossible that the blood of bulls and goats should
take away sin." Rom. 3:23-25, "Christ Jesus whom God
set forth to be a propitiation, through faith, in his blood, to
show his righteousness because of the passing over of the
sins done aforetime, in the forbearance of God." (2) Animal sacrifice was typical of the Supreme Sacrifice of the
Lamb of God. It "could only prefigure a life and a blood
that could truly, and justly, and honorably expiate sin"
(Campbell, **Christian System**, p. 51). The law had merely
"the shadow of the good things to come" (Heb. 10:1).
(3) Animal sacrifice was the substitute provided by Divine
grace for all the faithful, until such time as the actual and
all-sufficient Atonement should be mde. John 1:29—"Behold, the Lamb of God, that taketh away the sin of the
world!" The sublimity of this text is in the fact that here
the sins of all humanity are all bundled together and contemplated as a unit. Note well: "the sin of the world."
Gal. 4:4-6, "but when the fulness of the time came, God
sent forth his Son . . . that he might redeem them that were
under the law, that we might receive the adoption of sons."
Heb. 9:11-12, "but Christ . . . through his own blood, entered in once for all into the holy place, having obtained
eternal redemption for us." Heb. 9:26—"but now once
at the end of the ages hath he been manifested to put away
sin by the sacrifice of himself." Heb. 10:10—"we have
been sanctified through the offering of the body of Jesus
Christ once for all." (4) "The sacrifices of bulls and goats
were like token-money, as our paper-promises to pay, accepted at their face-value till the day of settlement. But the
sacrifice of Christ was the gold which absolutely extin-
guished all debt by its intrinsic value. Hence, when Christ
died, the veil that separated man from God was rent from
the top to the bottom by supernatural hands. When the

real expiation was finished, the whole symbolical system representing it became functum officio, and was abolished. Soon after this, the temple was razed to the ground, and the ritual was rendered forever impossible" (A. A. Hodge, **Popular Lectures**, p. 247).

64. Q. **What second principle of true religion did God establish through the Patriarchs?**

A. **The principle that acceptance with Him is always on the ground of faith.**

(1) Heb. 11:4—"by faith Abel offered unto God a more excellent sacrifice than Cain." Heb. 11:7—"By faith Noah . . . prepared an ark to the saving of his house." Heb. 11:8—"By faith Abraham . . . obeyed to go out unto a place which he was to receive for an inheritance." Heb. 11:13—"these all died in faith," etc. (2) Heb. 11:6— "without faith it is impossible to be well-pleasing unto him; for he that cometh to God must believe that he is, and that he is a rewarder of them that seek after him." Rom. 5:1— "being therefore justified by faith," etc.

65. Q. **What third essential principle of true religion did God establish through the Patriarchs?**

A. **The principle that true faith always manifests itself in works of faith, i. e., in obedience to the laws and commands of God.**

(1) Heb. 11, v. 4—by faith Abel offered a more excellent sacrifice. v. 7—by faith Noah built an ark to the saving of his house. v. 8—by faith Abraham obeyed to go out unto a place which he was to receive for an inheritance. v. 17—by faith Abraham offered up Isaac. (2) Jas. 2:21, 22—"Was not Abraham our father justified by works, in that he offered up Isaac his son upon the altar? Thou seest that faith wrought with his works, and by works was faith made perfect." (It should be explained that by "works" as the term is used here by James, is meant works of faith; not works of the moral law, such as Paul contemplates in Rom.

3:20, by which, he says, no flesh shall be justified). Faith that does not manifest itself in acts of faith, i. e. in obe' dience to the commands of God, is lifeless and impotent; it is mere intellectual assent to testimony, that is barren of beneficent results or accomplishments. Jas. 2:26—"For as the body apart from the spirit is dead, even so faith apart from works is dead."

66. Q. On what grounds, then, were the faithful souls of Patriarchal times accepted with God?

A. They were accepted on the ground of their faith which manifested itself in their obedience to the law of Sacrifice and to all the laws of God which were in force throughout the Patriarchal dispen- sation; and on the further ground of the cer- tainty of that Perfect Atonement for sin which was made once at the end of the ages.

(1) This Atonement was a matter of Divine decree. Acts 2:23—"him being delivered up by the determinate counsel and foreknowledge of God." This Atonement procured actual remission of sins for the faithful of all dispensations. See Gal. 4:4-5; Heb. 9:11-12; Heb. 9:26; Heb. 7:27; 1 Pet. 2:24, etc. (2) Although the faithful of the Patriarchal and Jewish dispensations did not actually receive the remission of their sins until Christ died on the Cross, yet they were obviously well-pleasing unto God and accepted with Him on the grounds stated above. Consequently, although they could not enter heaven in advance of Christ, yet they could and did, by virtue of the mercy extended to them on account of the Redeemer to come, prove themselves worthy of the divine inheritance and enter into it with Him. Heb. 9:15 —"And for this cause he is the mediator of a new covenant, that a death having taken place for the redemption of the transgressions that were under the first covenant, they that have been called may receive the promise of the eternal in- heritance." Eph. 4:8—"when he ascended on high, he led

captivity captive," etc. That some sort of an **intermediate** state was provided for these faithful souls of ancient times, until Christ came and died for them, is the view of some Christian scholars. Note, in this connection, the significance of the phrase, "Abraham's bosom," as used by Jesus, in Luke 16:22-23. However, we must always keep in mind that the kingdom (reign) of God is characterized by timelessness, and any attempt to apply our human measurements (chronology) to it is hardly warranted. (Cf. 2 Pet. 3:8.) With the God of the Bible there is no past, no future, but always the Everlasting Now (2 Cor. 6:2).

REVIEW EXAMINATION OVER LESSON
THIRTY-ONE

49. Q. What was the first revealed religion?
50. Q. What was the Patriarchal Religion?
51. Q. By what name are these men of faith of the most ancient times, known in the Scriptures?
52. Q. Where do we find the history of the Patriarchal Era?
53. Q. Who were the Patriarchs?
54. Q. What is the common designation for Patriarchal government and religion?
55. Q. What was the Patriarchal form of government?
56. Q. What was the Patriarchal form of religion?
57. Q. What three offices were administered by a Patriarch by divine authority?
58. Q. Who were the outstanding men of the Patriarchal Era?
59. Q. What fundamental institution of true religion did God establish through the Patriarchs?
60. Q. What fundamental ordinance of true religion did God establish through the Patriarchs?
61. Q. What first essential principle of true religion did God establish through the Patriarchs?
62. Q. Why did God require that sacrifice for sin should

include the shedding of blood?

63. Q. Does this mean that the ancients received actual remission of sins through animal sacrifices?

64. Q. What second principle of true religion did God establish through the Patriarchs?

65. Q. What third essential principle of true religion did God establish through the Patriarchs?

66. Q. On what grounds, then, were the faithful souls of Patriarchal times accepted with God?

Lesson Thirty-Two
WHAT GOD DID THROUGH ABRAHAM

Scripture Reading: Gen. 17:1-14, 22:15-18; Gal. 3:15-29.

Scripture to Memorize: "For ye are all sons of God, through faith, in Christ Jesus. For as many of you as were baptized into Christ did put on Christ. There can be neither Jew nor Greek, there can be neither bond nor free, there can be no male and female; for ye are all one man in Christ Jesus. And if ye are Christ's, then are ye Abraham's seed, heirs according to the promise" (Gal. 3:26-29).

67. Q. What was the Patriarchal Dispensation?

A. The Patriarchal Dispensation was that particular period in which God revealed His laws, established His institutions, and dispensed the benefits and blessings of His grace, through fathers or heads of families who were known as the Patriarchs.

(1) The **Standard Dictionary** defines a dispensation as "the particular way by which, at different periods, God has made known His dealings with mankind." (2) The history of Redemption, as recorded in the Holy Scriptures, extends over three dispensations, viz., the Patriarchal Dispensation, the Jewish or Mosaic Dispensation, and the Christian Dis-

pensation. The personal ministry of Jesus on earth was of course a special dispensation in itself.

68. Q. By what is the duration of a dispensation determined?

A. By the type of priesthood that prevails throughout the dispensation.

(1) The ordinance of Sacrifice required that sacrifice for sin should be offered to God alone; that it should be offered by man; and that it should be offered by a priest or by someone acting in the capacity of a priest. (2) In the Scriptures, the word priest denotes a person ordained and consecrated of God to offer sacrifices for his own sins and for the sins of the people, in which capacity he acted as mediator between God and man.

69. Q. What type of priesthood prevailed throughout the Patriarchal Dispensation?

A. The Patriarchal priesthood.

(1) During the Patriarchal era, the patriarch or father of the family acted as priest of his own household, and officiated at the domestic altar; and was succeeded at death by his firstborn son. (2) With the establishment of the Jewish or Mosaic Dispensation, the Patriarchal priesthood was set aside, and the Levitical (or Aaronic) priesthood was instituted. See Question 85. (3) In the present or Christian Dispensation, under the new covenant, all Christians are priests unto God, and Christ Himself is their High Priest. See 1 Pet. 2:5; Rev. 1:6, 5:10, 20:6; Heb. 7:16-17, 9:11-12, 9:24-28, etc. See Question 152. There is neither authority for, nor need of, a special human priesthood under the reign of the Holy Spirit.

70. Q. How did God make His laws known in Patriarchal times?

A. He communicated them to the Patriarchs who in turn handed them down to their posterity by word of mouth.

Gen. 2:16—"Jehovah God commanded the man, saying," etc. Gen. 7:1—"Jehovah said unto Noah," etc. Gen. 9:1— "God blessed Noah and his sons, and said unto them," etc. Gen. 12:1—"Jehovah said unto Abram," etc. Gen. 15:1— "the word of Jehovah came unto Abram in a vision, saying," etc. Gen. 22:1—"God did prove Abraham, and said unto him," etc.

71. Q. Who was perhaps the greatest of the Patriarchs?

A. Abraham, who, because of his great faith, is known in scripture as "the friend of God" and the father of all the faithful.

(1) Isa. 41:8—"the seed of Abraham my friend." Jas. 2:23—"he was called the friend of God." (2) Rom. 4:16 —"Abraham who is the father of us all," i. e., the children of God of both covenants. His name was originally Abram which means "exalted father" (Gen. 11:26, 12:1); later, it was changed to Abraham which means "father of a mul' titude" (Gen. 17:5).

72. Q. In what incident did Abraham especially demonstrate the greatness of his faith?

A. In the incident in which he showed his willingness to offer his son Isaac as a sacrifice, in obedience to God's command.

See Gen. 22. Here was an instance in which God's positive law ("Take now thy son . . . and get thee into the land of Moriah, and offer him there for a burnt-offering") super' seded His moral law (the law forbidding the taking of human life, Gen. 9:6, Exo. 20:13). No matter to what extent, however, the sentiment of filial affection may have protested against his doing the thing commanded, Abraham raised no questions, nor did he hesitate in the least, but acted in implicit obedience to the Divine command. Heb. 11:17-19, "By faith Abraham, being tried, offered up Isaac; yea, he that had gladly received the promises was offering up his only begotten son; even he to whom it is said, In

Isaac shall thy seed be called; accounting that God is able to raise up, even from the dead; from whence he did also in a figure receive him back."

73. Q. **What, firstly, did God do through Abraham?**

 A. **It was through Abraham that He originated the Hebrew people.**

(1) Gen. 12:2—"I will make of thee a great nation." Gen. 17:4—"thou shalt be the father of a multitude of nations." Gen. 22:17—"I will multiply thy seed as the stars of the heavens, and as the sand which is upon the seashore," etc. (2) It should be explained that Abraham was originally a Chaldean. When he first appears in the Bible narrative his home was in Ur of the Chaldeas (Gen. 11:28), a city of Mesopotamia near the source of the river Tigris. There God called him to go into Canaan and made him the pro-genitor of the Hebrew people.

74. Q. **What, secondly, did God do through Abraham?**

 A. **He originated and established the old covenant with Abraham and his posterity.**

(1) It should be explained here that the Bible consists of two parts, viz., the Old Testament Scriptures and the New Testament Scriptures. (2) The Old Testament Scriptures contain the record of the origination, establishment and de-velopment of the old covenant which God made with Abra-ham and his posterity, and which was mediated through Moses. The New Testament Scriptures reveal the princi-ples, laws and institutions of the new covenant, which God has made with all true believers, through the mediation of Jesus Christ.

75. Q. **What was the Abrahamic Promise?**

 A. **It is the name generally given to the four ele-mentary promises which God made to Abraham when He originated the old covenant through him.**

These promises were: (1) that Abraham should have a numerous offspring, Gen. 13:16, 15:3-5, 17:2-4, 22:17. (2) That God would be a God to him and to his seed after him, Gen. 17:1-8. (3) That He would give to Abraham and to his seed an everlasting possession, Gen. 12:7, 13:15, 15:18- 21, 17:8. (4) That He would bless all the nations of the earth through him and his seed, Gen. 12:3, 22:18.

76. **Q. In what manner was the Abrahamic Promise fulfilled?**

   A. It was fulfilled in a twofold manner; (1) literally, through the fleshly seed of Abraham, the Hebrew people; and (2) spiritually, through the spiritual seed of Abraham, the church of Christ.

(1) This twofold reference of the Abrahamic Promise may be described also as typical, and antitypical. "The first ele- ment, for instance, was a pledge to Abraham that he would have a numerous family, first, according to the flesh; and secondly, according to the Spirit; the second, that God would be a God to both of these families, though in a far higher sense to the latter than to the former; the third, that each of these families would become heirs to an inheritance; and the fourth, that through each of them the world would be blessed" (Milligan, **Scheme of Redemption**, p. 76). (2) Rom. 4:1-17, especially v. 16—"to the end that the promise may be sure to all the seed; not to that only which is of the law, but to that also which is of the faith of Abraham, who is the father of us all." Gal. 3:26-29, "For ye are all sons of God, through faith, in Christ Jesus. For as many of you as were baptized into Christ did put on Christ ... And if ye are Christ's then are ye Abraham's seed, heirs according to the promise." (3) The old covenant was a fleshly covenant; the new is a spiritual covenant, established upon better promises. See Jer. 31:31-34, 2 Cor. 3:1-14, Heb. 8:6-13, etc. (4) The fundamental difference between the old covenant and the new, is in the fact that those who

belonged to the old did so by virtue of the fact that the blood of Abraham flowed in their veins; whereas those who belong to the new, do so by virtue of the fact that they have the faith of Abraham in their hearts. The old cove-nant took in those born of Hebrew parents who were in-ducted into the covenant by circumcision when eight days old, and those servants who were bought with Hebrew money, proselyted and also inducted into the covenant by circumcision; in other words, infants and heathen servants who had to be taught to know God after their induction into the covenant. But the promise was that, under the new covenant, "they shall teach no more every man his neighbor, and every man his brother, saying, Know Jeho-vah; for they shall all know me, from the least of them unto the greatest of them, saith Jehovah." That is, they must be old enough to know God as He has revealed Him-self through Jesus Christ, before they are eligible for induc-tion into the new covenant. This is surely sufficient to convince any thinking person that infant church member-ship is not only unscriptural but impossible. See Gen. 17: 9-14, Jer. 31:31-34, Heb. 8:6-13. Those who would belong to the new covenant must be old enough to believe before they can be inducted into it. John 3:3—"Verily, verily, I say unto thee, except one be born anew, he cannot see the kingdom of God." Gal. 3:26—"For ye are all sons of God, through faith, in Christ Jesus." Rom. 5:1—"Being there-fore justified by faith we have peace with God through our Lord Jesus Christ."

77. Q. To whom did the Abrahamic Promise specifical-ly allude?

A. It alluded to Jesus Christ, who was the Seed of Abraham in a special sense.

That is, He was the Seed of Abraham, on His human side, through Mary. Gal. 3:7-8—"Know therefore that they that are of faith, the same are sons of Abraham. And the scripture, foreseeing that God would justify the Gentiles by faith, preached the gospel beforehand unto Abraham, saying, In thee shall all the nations be blessed." Gal. 3:16— "Now to Abraham were the promises spoken, and to his seed. He saith not. And to seeds, as of many; but as of one, And to thy seed, which is Christ." In other words, it is through Jesus Christ, who was the Seed of Abraham through the Virgin Mary, that the provisions of the Abrahamic Promise are being realized in their nobler, spiritual significations.

78.   Q.   What was the sign and seal of the old covenant which God originated through Abraham?

A.   Fleshly Circumcision.

See Gen. 17:9-14. The design of Circumcision was twofold: 1. "To separate Abraham and his posterity according to the flesh, from the rest of mankind, and thus to serve as a sign, seal, and token of the Old or National Covenant." 2. In its religious import, it was to typify "the cutting off of the body of sin from the soul, and the subsequent sealing of it by the Holy Spirit" (Milligan, ibid., pp. 80-81). See Rom. 2:28-29, Phil. 3:3, Col. 2:9-12, Eph. 1:13-14. Under the present dispensation, the indwelling Spirit is Himself the sign and seal of our inclusion in the new covenant. See Acts 2:38, 2 Cor. 1:21-22, Rom. 8:15-17, Eph. 1:13-14.

79.   Q.   What, then, do we find in the Old Testament Scriptures?

A.   We find the record of the unfolding of the literal or carnal side of the Abrahamic Promise, in the history of the Hebrew people.

80.   Q.   What do we find in the New Testament Scriptures?

A.   We find the record of the unfolding of the spiritual side of the Abrahamic Promise, in and through the spiritual family of Abraham, the church of Christ. Gal. 3:26-29.

81.   Q.   What great lesson do we learn from these truths?

      A.   That the subject-matter of the entire Bible is a
           unit; therefore the Bible must be of Divine origin.

No thinking person can become familiar with the internal
unity of the Bible as a whole, without realizing that it is a
book from God whose contents were revealed by inspiration of the Holy Spirit.

REVIEW EXAMINATION OVER LESSON
THIRTY-TWO

67.   Q.   What was the Patriarchal Dispensation?

68.   Q.   By what is the duration of a dispensation deter-
           mined?

69.   Q.   What type of priesthood prevailed throughout
           the Patriarchal Dispensation?

70.   Q.   How did God make His laws known in Patri-
           archal times?

71.   Q.   Who was perhaps the greatest of the Patriarchs?

72.   Q.   In what incident did Abraham especially demon-
           strate the greatness of his faith?

73.   Q.   What, firstly, did God do through Abraham?

74.   Q.   What, secondly, did God do through Abraham?

75.   Q.   What was the Abrahamic Promise?

76.   Q.   In what manner was the Abrahamic Promise
           fulfilled?

77.   Q.   To whom did the Abrahamic Promise specifical-
           ly allude?

78.   Q.   What was the sign and seal of the old covenant
           which God originated through Abraham?

79.   Q.   What, then, do we find in the Old Testament
           Scriptures?

80.   Q.   What do we find in the New Testament Scrip-
           tures?

81.   Q.   What great lesson do we learn from these truths?

Lesson Thirty-Three
WHAT GOD DID THROUGH MOSES

Scripture Reading: Heb. 11:24-29; 3:1-6.

Scriptures to Memorize: "And Moses indeed was faithful in all his house as a servant, for a testimony of those things which were afterward to be spoken; but Christ as a son, over his house, whose house are we, if we hold fast our boldness and the glorying of our hope firm unto the end" (Heb. 3:5-6). "For the law was given through Moses; grace and truth came through Jesus Christ" (John 1:17).

82. Q. **What was the institution of worship in the Patriarchal Dispensation?**

A. **The Altar.**

83. Q. **When did the Patriarchal Dispensation come to an end?**

A. **It came to an end when the Hebrew people were organized into a nation at Mount Sinai, under the leadership of Moses.**

84. Q. **What followed the Patriarchal Dispensation?**

A. **The Jewish or Mosaic Dispensation.**

85. Q. **What type of priesthood prevailed throughout the Jewish Dispensation?**

A. **The Levitical or Aaronic Priesthood.**

With the establishment of the Mosaic ritual, a particular order of men was appointed to the priesthood, with most solemn and imposing ceremonies; and from that time, the offering of sacrifices was restricted, in the main, to those who were duly invested with the priestly office. See Exo. 28, 2 Chron. 26:18. At the same time, the Altar was incorporated into the Tabernacle, and became known as the Altar of Burnt-Offering; and by this change it ceased to be a family altar and became a national altar. All the posterity of Aaron were, at this time, divinely appointed to be priests, except of course such as were disqualified by special pro-visions of the Mosaic Code. The office of High Priest was also established, and Aaron himself, the great-grandson of Levi and brother of Moses, was divinely designated to be the first man to occupy that exalted office (Exo. 6:16-20); and, by divine appointment also, the firstborn of the fami-ly, in direct descent and in regular succession from Aaron, came into incumbency of the office by divine right. The High Priest thus became the chief of the whole Jewish priesthood, and later the virtual head of the Jewish Theo-cracy. The Aaronic succession continued, despite numer-ous apostasies and captivities, down to the time of Jesus; and came to an end only with the destruction of Jerusalem by the Roman legions under Titus, A. D. 70, and the sub-sequent dispersion of the Jews among all nations.

86. Q. How is Moses described in the scripture records?

A. He is described as the great Lawgiver of Israel and the Mediator of the Old Covenant.

Gal. 3:19—"the law was ordained through angels by the hand of a mediator." John 1:17—"the law was given through Moses." John 7:19—"Did not Moses give you the law?" Cf. Exo. 20:18-21, Deut. 5:4-5.

87. Q. What, firstly, did God do through Moses?

A. It was through Moses that He organized the children of Israel into a nation and established the Theocracy.

A theocracy is defined as "a government of a state by the immediate direction of God"; hence the Hebrew common-wealth, before it became a kingdom, is usually referred to as a theocracy. The Old Sinaitic Covenant was essentially a national covenant, and the Mosaic Code was for both the civil and religious government of the nation. For purposes of comparison, the Decalogue or Ten Commandments might be said to correspond to our federal Constitution;

and the other laws, statutes and commandments of the Mosaic Code, to the body of statutory law by which our society is organized and its government administered. The
New Covenant, by way of contrast, is strictly spiritual, and
separate from the state in every particular. Jesus Himself
tells us to "render unto Caesar the things that are Caesar's,
and unto God the things that are God's" (Matt. 22:21).

**88. Q.   What were the outstanding features of the Mo-
saic Ritual?**

**A.   They were: (1) Circumcision, (2) the Passover,
(3) the Sabbath, (4) the Levitical Priesthood,
(5) the Tabernacle, (6) the Solemn Sacrifices,
and (7) the Solemn Feasts and Convocations.**

(These matters will be discussed in detail in a subsequent
lesson.)

89. Q.   Where is the Mosaic Code and Ritual revealed?

**A.   In the books of Exodus, Leviticus, Numbers and
Deuteronomy.**

90. Q.   What, secondly, did God do through Moses?

**A.   Through the mediation of Moses, He enlarged
the Abrahamic covenant into a national covenant, retaining Circumcision as the seal of the
covenant.**

Just four hundred and thirty years after the Promise was
given to Abraham (Gal. 3:17), its carnal or typical side
was fully developed in the Sinaitic or Old Covenant. Gen.
17:7—"I will establish my covenant between me and thee
and thy seed after thee throughout their generations" (the
words of Jehovah to Abraham when the Promise was
given). The Mosaic covenant and ritual was therefore, but
an enlargement of the Abrahamic covenant, which took in
Sacrifice, the essential ordinance of the Patriarchal system,
also. It will thus be seen that the whole procedure was a
progressive development of true religion.

91. Q. What, thirdly, did God do through Moses?

  A. It was through Moses that He revealed the eternal principles of right and wrong, in the provisions of the Decalogue or the Ten Commandments.

(This proposition will be treated in detail in Lesson Thirty-Four.)

92. Q. What is the Old Covenant or Mosaic System commonly designated in the apostolic writings?

  A. It is usually referred to as the Law.

The Mosaic System is so called because it was essentially a legal system. John 1:17—"For the law was given through Moses." John 7:10—"Did not Moses give you the law?" Gal. 3:24—"the law is become our tutor to bring us unto Christ."

93. Q. What were the successive institutions of worship under the Jewish Dispensation?

  A. The Tabernacle, the Temple, and the Synagogue.

(1) The Tabernacle began with Moses. God Himself gave Moses all the plans and specifications for it. See Exo. chs. 25-31. It was a portable institution adapted to the needs of the people during the period of their wanderings in the wilderness. (2) The Temple was built by Solomon, who received the idea and inspiration from his father David. See 2 Chron. chs. 1-7. The general design of the Tabernacle was carried out, on a grander scale of course, in the building of the Temple. The first Temple was built at Jerusalem, on Mount Moriah, about one thousand years before Christ. The Temple was designed to serve the people as a national institution of worship after they had become firmly established in Canaan. (3) The Synagogue began with Ezra, after the Exile. In purpose it was similar to our local churches; hence there was a synagogue in each community. Each synagogue served for a place of worship,

a law-court, and a school; and was presided over by local elders or "rulers" (Luke 13:14; Mark 5:22; Acts 13:15, 18:8).

94.   Q.   When did the Jewish Dispensation end?

A.   It ended with the death of Christ on the Cross. By His death He abrogated the Old Covenant, and at the same time ratified and established the New Covenant.

(1) Heb. 9:16—"For where a testament is, there must of necessity be the death of him that made it." Col. 2:14—"having blotted out the bond written in ordinances that was against us, which was contrary to us; and he hath taken it out of the way, nailing it to the cross." See also Jer. 31:31-34; Heb. 8:6-13; 2 Cor. 3, etc. (2) "The Old Sinaitic Covenant had to be taken out of the way, before a new covenant could be fully inaugurated as a separate and independent Institution. This was done at the death of Christ. Henceforth it was no longer binding on any one as a religious Institution; though it was, through the forbearance of God, allowed to remain as a civil and social Institution for about thirty-six years longer, until Jerusalem was destroyed by the Romans in A. D. 70" (Milligan, **Scheme of Redemption,** p. 78). (3) The New Covenant, moreover, was not merely an enlargement of the Old. It was distinctly a new covenant. Jer. 31:31—"I will make a new covenant," etc. Eph. 2:15, 16—"that he (Christ) might create in himself of the two (i. e., of Jew and Gentile) one new man, so making peace; and might reconcile them both in one body unto God through the cross." Note well: "one new man." Cf. Gal. 3:28, 1 Cor. 12:13, etc.

95.   Q.   On what grounds were the faithful souls of the Jewish Dispensation accepted with God?

A.   They were accepted on the ground of their faith which manifested itself in their obedience to the laws of God which were in force throughout the

Jewish Dispensation; and on the further ground
of the certainty of the Perfect Atonement for sin
which was made once at the end of the ages.

Deut. 7:12-13, "And it shall come to pass, because ye heark-
en to these ordinances, and keep and do them, that Jehovah
thy God will keep with thee the covenant and the loving
kindness which he sware unto thy fathers; and he will love
thee, and bless thee, and multiply thee," etc. See also Deut.
8:6-20; 28:1-6; 28:15-68; 30:1-10, etc. See also Neh. 9:9-
37, etc. Heb. 9:15—"And for this cause he is the mediator
of a new covenant, that a death having taken place for the
redemption of the transgressions that were under the first
covenant, they that have been called may receive the promise of the eternal inheritance." Gal. 4:4, 5—"But when
the fulness of the time came, God sent forth his Son, born
of a woman, born under the law, that he might redeem
them that were under the law, that we might receive the
adoption of sons." See Question 66.

REVIEW EXAMINATION OVER LESSON
THIRTY-THREE

82. Q. What was the institution of worship in the Patriarchal Dispensation?

83. Q. When did the Patriarchal Dispensation come to
an end?

84. Q. What followed the Patriarchal Dispensation?

85. Q. What type of priesthood prevailed throughout
the Jewish Dispensation?

86. Q. How is Moses described in the scripture records?

87. Q. What, firstly, did God do through Moses?

88. Q. What were the outstanding features of the Mosaic Ritual?

89. Q. Where is the Mosaic Code and Ritual revealed?

90. Q. What, secondly, did God do through Moses?

91. Q. What, thirdly, did God do through Moses?

92. Q.   What is the Old Covenant or Mosaic System commonly designated in the apostolic writings?
93. Q.   What were the successive institutions of worship under the Jewish Dispensation?
94. Q.   When did the Jewish Dispensation end?
95. Q.   On what grounds were the faithful souls of the Jewish Dispensation accepted with God?

Lesson Thirty-Four
THE DECALOGUE

Scripture Reading: Exo. 20:1-7; Matt. 19:16-22, 22:34-39.

Scripture to Memorize: "And he said unto him, Thou shalt love the Lord thy God with all thy heart, and with all thy soul, and with all thy mind. This is the great and first commandment. And a second like unto it is this, Thou shalt love thy neighbor as thyself. On these two commandments the whole law hangeth, and the prophets" (Matt. 22:37-40).

96. Q.   What is meant by the Decalogue?
    A.   By the Decalogue is meant the Ten Commandments.

97. Q.   What is the First Commandment?
    A.   It is: "Thou shalt have no other gods before me."

Exo. 20:3. Literally, before my face. This does not mean. Thou shalt put me above all other gods, as modern sophists have tried to make it appear to mean. It means, rather, Thou shalt not worship any other gods, or, Thou shalt have no other gods but Me. Cf. Deut. 6:13, 14—"Thou shalt fear Jehovah thy God, and him shalt thou serve ... Ye shall not go after other gods, of the gods of the peoples that are round about you." This command was directly against polytheism; and, indirectly against infidelity, heresy, materialism, skepticism, etc. Cf. Acts 14:15—"that ye should turn from these vain things unto a living God." Eph. 4:6—"one God and Father of all." Acts 17:24—"the God that made the world and all things therein," etc.

98. Q. What is the Second Commandment?

A. It is: "Thou shalt not make unto thee a graven image."

Exo. 20:4-6. This is a prohibition of image worship and idolatry; and, indirectly, of such sins as superstition, witch-craft, necromancy, and occultism (consorting with fortune-tellers and spirit mediums); of sacrilege (profanation of holy things); and of simony (using spiritual things for commercial ends). Cf. 1 John 5:21—"My little children, guard yourselves from idols."

99. Q. What is the Third Commandment?

A. It is: "Thou shalt not take the name of Jehovah thy God in vain."

Exo. 20:7. This is directed against swearing, blasphemy, cursing, breaking of religious vows, derision of religion, ir-reverence, perjury, etc. Cf. Matt. 5:34, the words of Jesus, "Swear not at all." Jas. 5:12—"but above all things, my brethren, swear not," etc.

100. Q. What is the Fourth Commandment?

A. It is: "Remember the sabbath day, to keep it holy."

Exo. 20:8-11. This command is not re-enacted in the New Testament, for the obvious reason that Christians have, from apostolic times, kept the first day of the week, the Lord's Day. The observance of the first day of the week was instituted and authorized by the apostles themselves, who were guided into all the truth by the Holy Spirit (John 16:13), as soon as the gospel was first proclaimed as fact and the first local churches were established. See Acts 20:7, 1 Cor. 16:2, Rev. 1:10. Under the old dispensation, the seventh day was set aside as the Sabbath, instead of the first, second, third, etc., day of the week, because that was the "day" on which God rested at the conclusion of His creative activity (Exo. 20-11). Moreover, the Sabbath itself was designed to be a memorial of the deliverance of the children of Israel from Egyptian bondage (Deut. 5:15) and would therefore have no significance for Gentiles. We as Christians keep the first day of the week, the Lord's Day, as a memorial of the resurrection of Jesus, which occurred on that day (Mark 16:9). Hence there is neither command nor precedent in the apostolic writings for Christians to keep the Jewish Sabbath. The Lord's Day is intended to be essentially a day of Christian worship, benevolence and service. We profane it exceedingly when we spend it in intemperance or debauchery, or in extravagant games, sports, amusements, revelings, and such like.

101.   Q.   What is the Fifth Commandment?

A.   It is: "Honor thy father and thy mother."

Exo. 20:12. This is directed against disrespect, irreverence, disobedience, etc., on the part of children towards their parents. Cf. Eph. 6:1—"Children, obey your parents in the Lord: for this is right." Cf. Eph. 6:4—"And ye fathers, provoke not your children to wrath; but nurture them in the chastening and admonition of the Lord."

102.   Q.   What is the Sixth Commandment?

A.   The Sixth Commandment is: "Thou shalt not kill."

(1) Exo. 20: 13. This is directed against the taking of human life in any form, such as homicide, suicide, infanticide, abortion, etc. How about "birth control," i. e., contraception? Is it the taking of incipient life? (2) This command does not apply of course in matters wherein we act as instruments of the state, as, for instance, in war, in the execution of criminals, or in protecting life from unjust attack; for we are commanded to "be in subjection to the higher powers," i. e., our civil rulers. See Rom. 13:1-7.

(3) This command is directed also against hatred, for, we are told, "whosoever hateth his brother is a murderer" (1 John 3:15); and against envy, quarreling, abusive words, imprecations, slander, scandalmongering, seduction, or any other practice that tends to destroy spiritual life. Cf. Rom. 13:9, 10—"Thou shalt not kill, Thou shalt not steal, Thou shalt not covet," etc.

103. Q. What is the Seventh Commandment?

A. It is: "Thou shalt not commit adultery."

Exo. 20:14. This is directed against adultery (illicit sexual intercourse between married persons, thus breaking the marriage vows); against fornication (illicit sexual inter' course between unmarried persons, or between one who is married and one who is unmarried); against sex perversion, sex abuse, sodomy, lasciviousness, lewdness, and all forms of sexual and social impurity. Cf. 1 Cor. 6:9-10, "neither fornicators, nor idolaters, nor adulterers, nor effeminate, nor abusers of themselves with men . . . shall inherit the kingdom of God." 1 Cor. 6:18—"Flee fornication." 1 Cor. 5:9—"have no company with fornicators." Cf. Rom. 1:26- 27; 2 Cor. 12:21; Gal. 5:19; Eph. 5:3-5; Col. 3:5; 1 Tim. 1:9-10, etc.

104. Q. What is the Eighth Commandment?

A. It is: "Thou shalt not steal."

Exo. 20:15. This is directed against robbery, theft, extor' tion, fraud, usury, etc. Cf. Eph. 4:28—"Let him that stole steal no more."

105. Q. What is the Ninth Commandment?

A. It is: "Thou shalt not bear false witness."

Exo. 20:16. This command is directed against lying, rail' ing, hypocrisy, detraction, calumny, false suspicion, and, in general, all sins by which the honor or character of our neighbor is injured. Cf. Col. 3:9—"lie not one to another." Eph. 4:25—"Wherefore, putting away falsehood, speak ye truth each one with his neighbor."

106. Q. What is the Tenth Commandment?

A. It is: "Thou shalt not covet."

Exo. 20:17. Covetousness is the most universal of all sins, yet seldom realized or admitted by the individual. The sins of envy and jealousy usually have their root in covetousness. This command is directed, therefore, against love of worldly goods, stinginess, God-robbery (Mal. 3:7-10), jealousy, envy, discontent, etc. The implication of the command is that we should be content with what we possess, and should not be envious of what belongs to others. Eph. 5:3—"covetousness, let it not even be named among you." Luke 12:15—here Jesus says: "Take heed, and keep yourselves from all covetousness: for a man's life consisteth not in the abundance of the things which he possesseth." Cf. Col. 3:5, 1 Cor. 5:11, Rom. 13:9-10, etc.

107. Q. What are the two greatest Commandments of the Law?

A. They are: the Command that we should love God wholeheartedly, and the Command that we should love our neighbors as ourselves.

(1) Deut. 6:4-5, Lev. 19:17-18, Matt. 22:35-40, "And one of them, a lawyer, asked him a question, trying him: Teacher, which is the greatest commandment in the law? And he said unto him, Thou shalt love the Lord thy God with all thy heart, and with all thy soul, and with all thy mind. This is the great and first commandment. And a second like unto it is this, Thou shalt love thy neighbor as thyself. On these two commandments the whole law hangeth, and the prophets." (2) These two Commandments, although not themselves included in the Decalogue, embrace within their scope, inferentially at least, all our obligations to God and all our obligations to our fellow-men. For this reason they are said to be the two greatest Commandments of the Law.

108. Q. Are the Ten Commandments binding upon

Christians, i. e., upon God's children under the New Covenant?

A.   They are all, with but one exception, binding upon Christians.

109.   Q.   Why are they binding upon Christians?

A.   They are binding upon Christians because they have been re-enacted, with but one exception, in the New Testament.

110.   Q.   Which one of the Ten Commandments has not been re-enacted in the New Testament and is therefore not binding upon Christians?

A.   The Fourth Commandment, i. e., the Commandment to keep the Sabbath, has not been re-enacted in the New Testament, and is therefore not binding upon Christians.

(This is fully explained under Question 100.)

111.   Q.   How were the Ten Commandments first revealed to the Hebrew people?

A.   The words of the Ten Commandments were spoken by Jehovah Himself to the children of Israel at Sinai.

Exo., chs. 19-20. The people were first required to wash their clothes, to sanctify themselves, in short, to make all necessary preparations to meet with God Almighty Himself. Two days were spent in ceremonies of purification and preparation for this sublime event. Then on the third day Moses brought forth the people out of the camp to meet God; and while the whole assembly stood at the foot of Sinai, God Himself descended to the summit of the holy mountain, in the midst of fire, with thunderings, lightnings, and the sound of a great trumpet. Exo. 19:18—"And mount Sinai, the whole of it, smoked, because Jehovah descended upon it in fire; and the smoke thereof ascended as the smoke of a furnace, and the whole mount quaked greatly." Then at length, while the people were greatly moved with awe, God spoke out of the midst of the fire, in such manner as to be heard by all the people, the sublime words of the Decalogue (Exo. 20:1-17). After the Decalogue was concluded, the people retired from the foot of the mountain, and requested that God henceforth communicate His words to them through Moses. This request was granted. The Ten Commandments were later written on two tablets of stone, which were delivered to the Israelites through Moses, to serve as their Fundamental Law. See Exo. 31:18, 32:1-20, 34:1-9, 34:27-35.

REVIEW EXAMINATION OVER LESSON THIRTY-FOUR

96. Q. What is meant by the Decalogue?
97. Q. What is the First Commandment?
98. Q. What is the Second Commandment?
99. Q. What is the Third Commandment?
100. Q. What is the Fourth Commandment?
101. Q. What is the Fifth Commandment?
102. Q. What is the Sixth Commandment?
103. Q. What is the Seventh Commandment?
104. Q. What is the Eighth Commandment?
105. Q. What is the Ninth Commandment?
106. Q. What is the Tenth Commandment?
107. Q. What are the two greatest Commandments of the Law?
108. Q. Are the Ten Commandments binding upon Christians, i. e., upon God's children under the New Covenant?
109. Q. Why are they binding upon Christians?
110. Q. Which one of the Ten Commandments has not been re-enacted in the New Testament and is therefore not binding upon Christians?
111. Q. How were the Ten Commandments first revealed to the Hebrew people?

Lesson Thirty-Five
WHY THE LAW WAS ADDED

Scripture Reading: Gal. 3:15-28; Rom. 7:1-6; Gal. 5:16-25.

Scriptures to Memorize: "What then is the law? it was added because of transgressions, till the seed should come to whom the promise hath been made; and it was ordained through angels by the hand of a mediator" (Gal. 3:19). "By the works of the law shall no flesh be justified in his sight; for through the law cometh the knowledge of sin" (Rom. 3:20). "For what the law could not do, in that it was weak through the flesh, God, sending His own Son in the likeness of sinful flesh, and for sin, condemned sin in the flesh; that the ordinance of the law might be fulfilled in us, who walk not after the flesh, but after the Spirit" (Rom. 8:3-4).

---

112. Q. What is meant by the Law in the scriptures quoted above?

A. By the Law is meant the entire Mosaic System. The Mosaic System is spoken of as the Law in all the apostolic writings, because it was essentially a legal system. The entire Old Covenant was a Covenant of Law. See John 1:17, 7:10.

113. Q. What was the purpose of the Mosaic Law?

A. It was "added because of transgressions, till the seed should come," Gal. 3:19.

(1) The Promise was given first, i. e., the Abrahamic Promise. Then the Law was added, i. e., added to the Promise. Furthermore, it was added "because of transgressions," i. e., on account of the rapid spread of sensualism, idolatry and moral corruption, it became necessary to reveal and establish the eternal principles of right and to distinguish the right from the wrong. This was done in and through the Law, particularly the Ten Commandments. It was add-

ed, moreover, till the Seed should come, i. e., Christ, who was Himself the fulfilment of the Law by His own perfect example of righteousness and holiness. Matt. 5:17—"Think not that I came to destroy the law or the prophets: I came not to destroy, but to fulfil." Hence, when He died on the Cross, the Law was abrogated as a covenant, and the Covenant of Grace was ushered in. John 1:17—"For the law was given through Moses; grace and truth came through Jesus Christ." (2) The design of the Old Covenant or the Covenant of Law was fourfold: 1. It was to serve as a civil and religious code for the government of the Hebrew nation. 2. It was added to convict and convince men of sin, by giving them a perfect rule of moral conduct. Rom. 3:20—"for through the law cometh the knowledge of sin." Rom. 7:7—"I had not known sin, except through the law; for I had not known coveting, except the law had said, Thou shalt not covet." 3. It was "to prevent the universal spread of idolatry, by preserving among men the knowledge and practice of true religion, till Christ should come." 4. Finally, the entire Old Covenant was for the purpose of giving to the world a pictorial outline of the Plan of Redemption as consummated in the Christian System, by means of certain types and symbols, rites and ceremonies, addressed as object lessons to men's physical senses. (See Milligan, **Scheme of Redemption**, pp. 83-85). Most of the characters, institutions and events of the Old Covenant were typical of Christ and His Church.

114. Q. What great truth did God reveal and establish through the Mosaic System?

A. The truth that the law is inadequate to save men from their sins.

(1) Law is not designed to make us better men and women, nor can it possibly make us more spiritually-minded. Its function is to define what is right, and to distinguish right from wrong. Its penalty is for the purpose of restraining

the lawless. Therefore law is inadequate to save men from their sin. Rom. 3:20—"by the works of the law shall no flesh be justified in his sight; for through the law cometh the knowledge of sin." 1 Cor. 15:56—"the sting of death is sin; and the power of sin is the law." (2) A person may keep the moral law diligently and circumspectly, and still fall far short of salvation. Hence the folly of expecting to be saved on the ground of respectability, of being a good citizen, a moral man, etc. Salvation is not on the ground of obedience to the moral law, but is a gift of God to be accepted and appropriated on our part by the obedience of faith. (See Question 14). Law merely defines and points out sin, and provides the penalty; hence it is wholly inadequate to remove the guilt of sin. (3) Hence what the Law could not do for man, God did for him, in that out of His divine grace He provided a Savior for him, who is able to save him from his sins. Rom. 8:3—"For what the law could not do, in that it was weak through the flesh, God, sending his own Son in the likeness of sinful flesh, and for sin, condemned sin in the flesh." (4) It follows, therefore, that if men reject the only Sacrifice for sin which God has provided, the Lamb of God Himself, they are without promise and without hope; for the simple reason that there is no other Sin-offering, no other Atonement, no other means of salvation. John 14:6—"no one cometh unto the Father, but by me." Salvation is through Christ alone; no human being was ever pardoned except on the merits of Christ's atoning blood.

115. Q. Are the Ten Commandments binding upon us who live in the Christian Dispensation and under the New Covenant?

A. Those which have been re-enacted in the New Testament are binding upon us.

(1) A testament is a will. God has made two wills. The old was made with reference to the fleshly seed of Abra-

ham, through the mediation of Moses. The new is made with reference to all true believers, through the mediation of Jesus Christ: and is therefore known as "The Last Will and Testament of Our Lord and Saviour Jesus Christ." (2) It is a well-known principle of law that a final will abro-gates and supersedes all previous wills that may have been made. Therefore, we who live in the Christian Dispensa-tion are under the provisions of the New Testament. (3) Oftentimes when a man makes two wills, he will take cer-tain provisions of the old will and incorporate them in his new will. Those provisions become binding, not because they were in the old will, but because they have been re-enacted in the new will. Consequently the moral principles embodied in the Ten Commandments, which have been re-enacted in the New Testament, are binding upon us, not because they were in the Old Testament, but because they are re-enacted in the New. (4) As shown in Lesson Thirty-Four, all the Commandments, or the moral princi-ples embodied in them, have been re-enacted in the apostolic writings, with but one exception. (See Gal. 5:19-21, Eph. 5:3-5, 1 Cor. 6:9-10, Rev. 21:8, 22:15, etc.) The sole ex-ception is the Fourth Commandment. There is no com-mand in the New Testament Scriptures that Christians should keep the Sabbath. As previously explained, we as Christians are divinely authorized to keep the first day of the week, the Lord's Day. The other Commandments have been re-enacted in the New Testament, however, and are therefore binding upon us.

116. Q. Will the keeping of the Ten Commandments make one a Christian or procure salvation for anyone under the New Covenant?

A. No. We cannot be Christian if we do not ear-nestly strive to keep the Commandments; but, on the other hand, we may keep all the Com-mandments and fall short of salvation, for the

simple reason that salvation is only through Christ, and must be accepted on our part by faith in Him.

As the moral principles embodied in the Ten Commandments have been incorporated in the civil law of all civilized nations, it follows that one must obey the Commandments in order to keep out of jail. On the other hand, we may obey all the Commandments, and still not be Christians; for there is nothing in the Ten Commandments about Christ, the gospel, the church, etc. We could keep the Commandments and not even know about Christ, not believe in Him, not accept Him as our Saviour, not be baptized, not observe the Lord's Supper, in fact not keep any of the appointments essential to our salvation and growth in holiness. Therefore the Ten Commandments are wholly inadequate so far as the matter of procuring salvation for anyone is concerned. For a clear illustration of this truth, see the story of the rich young ruler, Matt. 19:16-22, Mark 10:17-22, Luke 18:18-30.

117. Q. **What great lesson should we derive from these truths?**

A. **We should learn that salvation is not a reward which we can merit by our obedience to the moral law, but that it is a gift which can be received only through our faith in Christ and appropriated only through our obedience to His commands and appointments.**

John 14:1—"ye believe in God, believe also in me." John 14:6—"Jesus said unto him, I am the way, and the truth, and the life: no one cometh unto the Father, but by me." Rom. 3:20—"by the works of the law shall no flesh be justified in his sight." Eph. 2:8—"for by grace have ye been saved through faith; and that (salvation) not of yourselves, it is the gift of God." Tit. 3:5—"Not by works done in righteousness, which we did ourselves, but according to his mercy he saved us." Rom. 6:23—"For the wages of sin is death; but the free gift of God is eternal life in Christ Jesus our Lord."

REVIEW EXAMINATION OVER LESSON
THIRTY-FIVE

112. Q. What is meant by the Law in the scriptures quoted above?

113. Q. What was the purpose of the Mosaic Law?

114. Q. What great truth did God reveal and establish through the Mosaic System?

115. Q. Are the Ten Commandments binding upon us who live in the Christian Dispensation and under the New Covenant?

116. Q. Will the keeping of the Ten Commandments make one a Christian or procure salvation for anyone under the New Covenant?

117. Q. What great lesson should we derive from these truths?

Lesson Thirty-Six

WHAT GOD DID THROUGH THE HEBREW
PROPHETS

Scripture Reading: 1 Pet. 1:3-12.

Scriptures to Memorize: "God, having of old time spoken unto the fathers in the prophets by divers portions and in divers manners" (Heb. 1:1). "For no prophecy ever came by the will of man; but men spake from God, being moved by the Holy Spirit" (2 Pet. 1:21).

118. Q. Who were the Prophets?

A. The Prophets were men specially called and enlightened by God, to reveal His communications to the Hebrew people and their rulers, particularly throughout the centuries of religious apostasy and national decay.

The Prophets were both evangelists and reformers. They were the revealers of God's will, historians of the nation, instructors of the people, privy counselors to their kings, zealous upholders of true religion, and denouncers of sin in all its forms. They were also foretellers of the various details of the life and work and reign of the coming Messiah. They were preachers of personal holiness, national righteous‐ ness, and social justice. For pure devotion, zeal, fearless‐ ness, and spiritual passion, the Prophets were the outstand‐ ing leaders of all Hebrew history.

119. Q. Who was the first of the great Prophets?

A. Samuel, the founder of the School of the Prophets.

See Acts 3:24; 1 Sam. 10:5‐10, 19:20; 2 Ki. 2:3, 2:5, 4:38, etc.

120. Q. Name the great Hebrew Prophets.

A. They were: Samuel, Elijah, Elisha, Isaiah, Jere‐ miah, Ezekiel, Daniel, and John the Baptizer.

121. Q. Name the lesser Hebrew Prophets.

A. They were: Hosea, Joel, Amos, Obadiah, Jonah, Micah, Nahum, Habakkuk, Zephaniah, Haggai, Zechariah, and Malachi.

122. Q. What special work did God do through the Hebrew Prophets?

A. He handed down through them a series of pre‐ dictions covering all the circumstances of the entrance of the Word into human flesh and His dwelling among men as their Messiah and Redeemer.

The Prophets foretold that the Messiah would be born of a virgin (Isa. 7:13‐14, Mic. 5:3; Matt. 1:18‐25, Luke 1:26‐ 35); that He would be born in Bethlehem, the city of

David (Mic. 5:2, Matt. 2:1-11; Luke 2:1-7, John 7:40-42);
that a forerunner would prepare the world for His advent.
(Mal. 3:1-2, 4:5-6; Isa. 40:3; John 1:22-23; Mark 1:1-7;
Matt. 3:1-3, 11:9-11); that He would possess the Holy
Spirit without measure (Isa. 11:1-9; John 3:34); that His
ministry would be authenticated by miracles of mercy (Isa.
42:1-7, Acts 10:38); that He would be betrayed by one of
His own disciples (Psa. 41:9; Mark 14:43-49; John 18:1-5);
that the betrayer would return the thirty pieces of silver,
the price of His betrayal (Zech. 11:12-13; Matt. 27:3-10);
that another would be chosen to fill the betrayer's place
(Psa. 109:8; Acts 1:15-20); that His followers would for-
sake Him in His hour of peril and suffering (Zech. 13:7;
Matt. 26:31-56); that He would be scourged, mocked and
abused (Isa. 50:6; John 19:1; Mark 14:65; Matt. 27:27-31);
that He would suffer in silence, as the sacrificial Lamb of
God (Isa. 53:4-7; John 1:29; Mark 15:2-5; Acts 8:32-35);
that He would be crucified, and His hands and feet pierced
(Psa. 22:16; Luke 23:33; Zech. 12:10, 13:6; Acts 2:22, 23,
27); that vinegar and gall would be given Him to drink
(Psa. 69:20-21; Matt. 27:33-34); that His executioners
would divide His garments (Psa. 22:18; John 19:23-24);
that He would endure the Cross even unto death (Psa.
22:1-21; Matt. 27:46; Luke 24:25-27; Acts 26:22-23); that
He would die (Isa. 53:8; Luke 23:46); that He would
make His grave with both the wicked and the rich (Isa.
53:9; Matt. 27:38, 27:57-60); that not a bone of His body
would be broken (Psa. 34:20; John 19:32-36); that He
would be raised up from the dead (Psa. 16:10; Psa. 17:15;
Jonah 1:17; Matt. 12:39-40; John 2:19-22; Luke 24:1-7;
Acts 13:34-37, 2:23-27; 1 Cor. 15:1-4); that He would
ascend to the Father in heaven (Psa. 8:5-6; 110:1; Luke
24:50-53; Acts 1:9-11; Eph. 4:8-10; Heb. 12:2); that He
would be crowned King of kings and Lord of lords (Psa.
24:7-10; Psa. 2:6; Acts 2:33; Phil. 2:9-11; 1 Tim. 6:15);
that He would send the Holy Spirit, according to promise,

to carry on His work in the world (Joel 2:28-29; Acts 2:1-33, 4:31; John 15:26-37, 14:16-17).

123. Q. **What was the purpose of these Messianic predictions?**

A. **They were for the purpose of identifying the true Messiah when He should appear among men.**

(1) These predictions were made over a period extending from some one thousand years to three hundred years before Christ. It follows, therefore, that the One in whose life and ministry and work these predictions were all fulfilled, was, beyond all reasonable doubt, the true Messiah. This One was Jesus of Nazareth, our Redeemer, our High Priest, and our King. (2) Prophecy and its fulfilment is another incontrovertible proof of the Divine origin of the Scriptures. 2 Pet. 1:21—"For no prophecy ever came by the will of man; but men spake from God, being moved by the Holy Spirit." 1 Pet. 1:10, 11—"Concerning which salvation the prophets sought and searched diligently, who prophesied of the grace that should come unto you: searching what time or what manner of time the Spirit of Christ which was in them did point unto, when it testified beforehand the sufferings of Christ, and the glories that should follow them."

124. Q. **Who was the last of the great Hebrew Prophets?**

A. **John the Baptizer.**

See Matt. 3:1-6; Mal. 4:5-6; Matt. 11:11-14; Mark 9:11-13, Luke 1:13-17.

125. Q. **What was the specific work of John the Baptizer?**

A. **He was sent to call the Jewish nation to repentance, and to herald the appearance of the Messiah.**

See Matt. 3:1-17; Mark 1:1-8; Luke 1:13-17; 3:1-22; John 1:19-34; Isa. 40:3; Mal. 3:1-2, 4:5-6.

REVIEW EXAMINATION OVER LESSON THIRTY-SIX

118. Q. Who were the Prophets?
119. Q. Who was the first of the great Prophets?
120. Q. Name the great Hebrew Prophets.
121. Q. Name the lesser Hebrew Prophets.
122. Q. What special work did God do through the Hebrew Prophets?
123. Q. What was the purpose of these Messianic predictions?
124. Q. Who was the last of the great Hebrew Prophets?
125. Q. What was the specific work of John the Baptizer?

Lesson Thirty-Seven

WHAT GOD DID THROUGH THE HEBREW PEOPLE

Scripture Reading: 1 Cor. 10:1-13.

Scriptures to Memorize: "For whatsoever things were written aforetime were written for our learning, that through patience and through comfort of the scriptures we might have hope" (Rom. 15:4). "So that the law is become our tutor to bring us unto Christ, that we might be justified by faith. But now that faith is come, we are no longer under a tutor" (Gal. 3:24-25).

126. Q. Why did not God send His Son into the world to save the world immediately after the fall of our first parents?
      A. Evidently because considerable time was neces-

sary in order to prepare Christianity for mankind, and to prepare mankind for the reception and enjoyment of Christianity.

Why did the Redeemer wait four thousand years and more, before He came into the world to suffer and die for us and to save us from our sins? Why was not the kingdom established in its fulness immediately after man's expulsion from the Garden of Eden? To these questions, we might counter with the following: Why did not God so constitute the acorn that it would grow into an oak instantaneously? Or, why has He not so constituted an infant that it will grow into a man or woman in a few minutes, or in a few weeks or months? None of these questions is so easily answered. It seems, however, that "sundry matters had first to be practically demonstrated before the Gospel could be fully and properly revealed to mankind as the power of God for the salvation of every true believer" (Milligan, **Scheme of Redemption,** p. 73).

127. Q. **What proposition was left to the Gentiles to demonstrate, in preparing the world for Christianity?**

A. **It was left to the Gentiles to demonstrate the inadequacy of Natural Religion to meet and supply the wants of our fallen race.**

This proposition the Gentiles demonstrated by their numerous failures in theoretical and practical morality, such as, for instance, Platonism, Aristotelianism, Stoicism, Epicureanism, Cynicism, etc., and all forms of Philosophy; and by their equally numerous failures in trying to establish an adequate system of religion with only the dim light of Nature to guide them. This matter is fully discussed in Questions 22, 23, and 24. Rom. 1:20-32, "For the invisible things of him since the creation of the world are clearly seen, being perceived through the things that are made, even his everlasting power and divinity; that they may be without excuse: because that, knowing God, they glorified him not as God, neither gave thanks; but became vain in their reasonings, and their senseless heart was darkened. Professing themselves to be wise, they became fools, and changed the glory of the incorruptible God for the likeness of an image of corruptible man, and of birds, and four-footed beasts, and creeping things." The reference here is to animal worship, and even insect worship, which prevailed among the ancient heathen peoples. Continuing: "Wherefore God gave them up in the lusts of their hearts unto uncleanness, that their bodies should be dishonored among themselves: for that they exchanged the truth of God for a lie, and worshipped and served the creature rather than the Creator, who is blessed for ever. Amen. For this cause God gave them up unto vile passions: for their women changed the natural use into that which is against nature; and likewise also the men, leaving the natural use of the women, burned in their lust one toward another, men with men working unseemliness, and receiving in themselves that recompense of their error which was due." The reference here is to the degrading sexual practices which prevailed among the ancients, such as abortion, sodomy, sex perversion, etc., and which prevail all too generally even in our day. Continuing: "And even as they refused to have God in their knowledge, God gave them up unto a reprobate mind, to do those things which are not fitting; being filled with all unrighteousness, wickedness, covetousness, maliciousness; full of envy, murder, strife, deceit, malignity; whisperers, backbiters, hateful to God, insolent, haughty, boastful, inventors of evil things, disobedient to parents, without understanding, covenant-breakers, without natural affection, unmerciful; who, knowing the ordinance of God, that they that practise such things are worthy of death, not only do the same, but also consent with them that practise them." This entire section is a scathing delineation and denunciation of the sins of heathendom. See also 1 Cor.

1:21—"For seeing that in the wisdom of God the world through its wisdom knew not God, it was God's good pleasure through the foolishness of the preaching to save them that believe." How utterly absurd, then for any human being to attempt to apprehend and know and worship God rightly from the revelation of Nature! How true, by way of contrast, the words of Jesus: "He that hath seen me hath seen the Father" (John 14:9).

128. Q. What, firstly, did God do through the Hebrew people?

A. Through the Hebrew people, He perpetuated and increased the knowledge of Himself, His attributes and His works, among men.

Through the Patriarchs, He revealed His selfexistence, His unity, His personality, His spirituality and His benevolence. Through Moses and the demonstrations in Egypt and in the Wilderness, He revealed His Omnipotence. Through the Prophets especially, He revealed His wisdom and holiness. And throughout the entire history of the Hebrew people, He revealed His infinite justice, righteousness, and compassion.

129. Q. What, secondly, did God do through the Hebrew people?

A. Through the Hebrew people, He perpetuated and developed the essential principles, laws and institutions of true religion.

Those elements of true religion are, as we have learned: Altar, Sacrifice and Priesthood.

130. Q. What, thirdly, did God do through the Hebrew people?

A. Through them He revealed the essential principles of moral conduct, and of national and social righteousness.

The principles of moral conduct, i. e., of right and wrong,

"for through the law cometh the knowledge of sin." Eccl.
12:13—"Fear God, and keep his commandments; for this
is the whole duty of man." Pro. 14:34—"Righteousness
exalteth a nation; but sin is a reproach to any people." Psa.
111:10—"The fear of Jehovah is the beginning of wisdom;
a good understanding have they that do his command'
ments." The Prophets were outstanding advocates of social
justice and national righteousness. Amos 5:11—"Foras'
much therefore as ye trample upon the poor, and take exac'
tions from him of wheat: ye have built houses of hewn
stone, but ye shall not dwell in them," etc. Amos. 5:14—
"Seek good, and not evil, that ye may live," etc. Isa. 1:15'
17, "And when ye spread forth your hands, I will hide
mine eyes from you; yea, when ye make many prayers, I
will not hear: our hands are full of blood. Wash you, make
you clean; put away the evil of your doings from before
mine eyes; cease to do evil; learn to do well; seek justice,
relieve the oppressed, judge the fatherless, plead for the
widows." Jer. 25:5'6, "Return ye now every one from his
evil way, and from the evil of your doings, and dwell in
the land that Jehovah hath given unto you and to your
fathers, from of old and even for evermore; and go not
after other gods to serve them, and to worship them, and
provoke me not to anger with the work of your hands:
and I will do you no hurt."

131.   Q.   What, fourthly, did God do through the He-
            brew people?

       A.   Through them especially He made known the
            inadequacy of Law to save people from their
            sins.

Rom. 8:3—"For what the law could not do, in that it was
weak through the flesh, God, sending his own Son in the
likeness of sinful flesh and for sin, condemned sin in the
flesh." Heb. 10:1—"For the law having a shadow of good
things to come, not the very image of the things, can never

with the same sacrifices year by year, which they offer continually, make perfect them that draw nigh." The Hebrew people were specially called and used of God to demonstrate the exceeding sinfulness of sin, our inability to save ourselves through works of the moral law, and consequently the need on our part of personal regeneration and holiness.

132.   Q.   What, fifthly, did God do through the Hebrew people?

   A.   Through them He built up a system of type, symbol and prophecy, designed to identify the true Messiah at His coming, and to establish the divine origin of the entire Christian System.

1 Cor. 10:11—"Now these things happened unto them by way of example; and they were written for our admonition, upon whom the ends of the ages are come." Rom. 15:4— "For whatsoever things were written aforetime were written for our learning, that through patience and through comfort of the scriptures we might have hope." Heb. 10:1 —"For the law having a shadow of good things to come," etc. Most of the characters, institutions and events of the Old Covenant were typical of Christ and His Church. Adam, Isaac, Joseph, Moses, Joshua, David, Jonah, etc., were all types of Christ. The deliverance of Noah from the ungodly antediluvian world, through water, was typical of our deliverance from the bondage and corruption of sin, through baptism, water in each case being the transitional element through which deliverance is wrought (1 Pet. 3:20-21). The Tabernacle and the Temple were both types of the Church. The Paschal Lamb, the Smitten Rock, The Brazen Serpent, etc., were typical of Christ. The Levitical Priesthood was typical of the priesthood of all Christians. Canaan was a type of Heaven. In fact the entire Mosaic System was, in its essential features, typical of the Christian System. Typology is a most convincing proof of

the divine origin of the Scriptures, for it must be admitted that the points of resemblance between the types and their corresponding antitypes were designed and preordained by the same God who established them and revealed them through His Holy Spirit. We may rightly say, therefore, that

The Old Testament is the New Testament concealed,
And the New Testament is the Old Testament revealed.

REVIEW EXAMINATION OVER LESSON THIRTY-SEVEN

126.   Q.   Why did not God send His Son into the world to save the world immediately after the fall of our first parents?

127.   Q.   What proposition was left to the Gentiles to demonstrate, in preparing the world for Christianity?

128.   Q.   What, firstly, did God do through the Hebrew people?

129.   Q.   What, secondly, did God do through the Hebrew people?

130.   Q.   What, thirdly, did God do through the Hebrew people?

131.   Q.   What, fourthly, did God do through the Hebrew people?

132.   Q.   What, fifthly, did God do through the Hebrew people?

Lesson Thirty-Eight

WHAT GOD DID THROUGH HIS SON JESUS CHRIST

Scripture Reading: John 14:1-10.

Scriptures to Memorize: "God, having of old time spoken unto the fathers in the prophets by divers portions and in divers manners, hath at the end of these days spoken unto us in his Son" (Heb. 1:1-2). "God was in Christ reconciling the world unto himself" (2 Cor. 5:19). "He that hath seen me hath seen the Father" (John 14:9).

---

133.   Q.   What, firstly, did God do through His Son Jesus Christ?

A.   Through Jesus Christ God revealed Himself to mankind.

(1) Heb. 1:1, 2—"God ... hath at the end of these days spoken unto us in his Son." John 1:18—"No man hath seen God at any time; the only begotten Son, who is in the bosom of the Father, he hath declared him." John 12:45— "he that beholdeth me beholdeth him that sent me." John 14:9—"he that hath seen me hath seen the Father." (2) If you would listen to the wisdom of God, hear, study, meditate upon the teaching of Jesus. No human being has ever been able to add one moral or spiritual truth to the body of teaching which He left in the world. John 7:46— "Never man so spake." Matt. 7:28—"the multitudes were astonished at his teaching," etc. (3) If you would know something of the holiness of God, contemplate the matchless purity of Jesus, who not only gave a perfect teaching, but a perfect example as well. John 8:46—"which of you convicteth me of sin?" He made the will of His heavenly Father the supreme rule of conduct in His life. John 4:34— "My meat is to do the will of him that sent me, and to accomplish his work." And to the last moment of His incarnate life, even during His agony in the garden, the burden of His prayer was, always, "nevertheless not my will, but thine, be done" (Luke 22:42). (4) If you would see the power of God contemplate all the "mighty works and wonders and signs which God did by him" (Acts 2:22). In this connection, note the wide variety of His miracles as to kind, such as, the feeding of a multitude with a few

loaves and fishes, the turning of water into wine, the cursing of the fig tree, the stilling of the tempest, the casting
out of demons, the healing of the sick of all manner of
diseases, and the raising of the dead. He had but to speak,
and all Nature obeyed His voice. Matt. 8:27—"and the
men marvelled, saying, What manner of man is this, that
even the winds and the sea obey him?" (5) If you would
comprehend the love of God for man, behold the Sacrificial
Lamb suffering upon Calvary's tree, the innocent for the
guilty, offering Himself voluntarily and freely for the sins
of the whole world. Isa. 53:5—"He was wounded for our
transgressions, he was bruised for our iniquities; the chastisement of our peace was upon him; and with his stripes
we are healed." John 15:13—"Greater love hath no man
than this, that a man lay down his life for his friends." 1
John 4:10—"Herein is love, not that we loved God, but
that he loved us, and sent his Son to be the propitiation
for our sins."

134.   Q.   What, secondly, did God do through His Son
                Jesus Christ?

         A.   Through Jesus Christ He gave to all mankind
                a Perfect Pattern of living, a Perfect Example
                of righteousness and holiness.

Heb. 4:15—"For we have not a high priest that cannot be
touched with the feeling of our infirmities; but one that
hath been in all points tempted like as we are, yet without
sin." Heb. 7:26—"For such a high priest became us, holy,
guileless, undefiled, separated from sinners, and made higher
than the heavens." etc. Because of His personal purity,
God has presented Him to us as our only Leader and Exemplar in the conflict of life. Isa. 55:4—"Behold, I have given
him for a witness to the peoples, a leader and commander
to the peoples." Matt. 17:5—"This is my beloved Son, in
whom I am well pleased; hear ye him." Eph. 5:1, 2—"Be
ye therefore imitators of God, as beloved children; and

walk in love, even as Christ also loved you, and gave himself up for us." 1 Thess. 1:6—"And ye became imitators
of us, and of the Lord." Heb. 12:1, 2—"Therefore let us
also ... lay aside every weight, and the sin which doth so
easily beset us, and let us run with patience the race that
is set before us, looking unto Jesus the author and perfecter
of our faith, who for the joy that was set before him en-
dured the cross, despising shame, and hath sat down at the
right hand of the throne of God." One reason why the
Word became flesh and dwelt among us (John 1:14) was,
that He might show us by His example how we should live
and walk in order to please God.

**135. Q. What, thirdly, did God do through His Son
Jesus Christ?**

**A. In Jesus Christ God provided an all-sufficient
Atonement for the sins of the whole world.**

(This subject will be treated fully in Lesson Thirty-Nine.)

**136. Q. What, fourthly, did God do through His Son
Jesus Christ?**

**A. Through Jesus Christ He ratified and established
the New Covenant, the Covenant of Grace,
with its essential principles, laws, institutions,
blessings, and rewards.**

(1) The New Covenant was ratified when Christ died on
the Cross. Heb. 8:6—"But now hath he obtained a ministry the more excellent, by so much as he is also the mediator of a better covenant, which hath been enacted upon
better promises." Heb. 9:15-16, "And for this cause he is
the mediator of a new covenant, that a death having taken
place for the redemption of the transgressions that were
under the first covennt, they that have been called may
receive the promise of the eternal inheritance. For where
a testament is, there must of necessity be the death of him
that made it." (2) The New Covenant is the Covenant of
Grace. Rom. 8:3—"For what the law could not do, in

that it was weak through the flesh, God, sending his own Son in the likeness of sinful flesh and for sin, condemned sin in the flesh." John 1:17—"For the law was given through Moses; grace and truth came through Jesus Christ." Rom. 6:14—"For sin shall not have dominion over you: for ye are not under law, but under grace." Rom. 5:21— "that, as sin reigned in death, even so might grace reign through righteousness unto eternal life through Jesus Christ our Lord." (3) The New Covenant is the Gospel Cove-nant. 1 Cor. 15:1-4, "Now I make known unto you, breth-ren, the gospel which I preached unto you ... For I de-livered unto you first of all that which also I received: that Christ died for our sins according to the scriptures; and that he was buried; and that he hath been raised on the third day according to the scriptures." Rom. 1:16—"For I am not ashamed of the gospel, for it is the power of God unto salvation to every one that believeth; to the Jew first, and also to the Greek."

137. Q. What, fifthly, did God do through his Son Jesus Christ?

A. Through Jesus Christ He achieved the conquest of death and procured for His saints the hope and certainty of a glorious immortality.

Acts 2:32—"This Jesus did God raise up, whereof we are all witnesses." Acts 10:40—"Him God raised up the third day." John 11:25, 26—"I am the resurrection, and the life ... whosoever liveth and believeth on me shall never die." 2 Tim. 1:10—"our Savior Christ Jesus, who abolished death, and brought life and immortality to light through the gospel." Rom. 8:11—"he that raised up Christ Jesus from the dead shall give life also to your mortal bodies through his Spirit that dwelleth in you." Phil. 3:20, 21— "the Lord Jesus Christ, who shall fashion anew the body of our humiliation, that it may be conformed to the body of his glory." Our Lord Jesus Christ proposes to redeem us not only from the bondage of sin, but from the bondage of death as well. Rom. 8:23—"we ourselves groan within ourselves, waiting for our adoption, to wit, the redemption of our body." Cf. also 1 Cor. 15:35-57.

138.   Q.   **What, finally, does God propose to do through His Son Jesus Christ?**

A.   **He proposes nothing short of the complete purging of our world of all the works of the devil.**

Heb. 2:14, 15—"Since then the children are sharers in flesh and blood, he also himself in like manner partook of the same; that through death he might bring to nought him that had the power of death, that is, the devil; and might deliver all them who through fear of death were all their lifetime subject to bondage." 1 John 3:8—"To this end was the Son of God manifested, that he might destroy the works of the devil." 1 Cor. 15:25, 26—"For he must reign, till he hath put all enemies under his feet. The last enemy that shall be abolished is death." Rev. 20:10—"And the devil that deceived them was cast into the lake of fire and brimstone, where are also the beast and the false proph-et; and they shall be tormented day and night for ever and ever." Rev. 20:14—"And death and Hades were cast into the lake of fire." Rev. 21:4—"and death shall be no more." 2 Pet. 3:13—"But, according to promise, we look for new heavens and a new earth, wherein dwelleth righteousness."

REVIEW EXAMINATION OVER LESSON THIRTY-EIGHT

133.   Q.   What, firstly, did God do through His Son Jesus Christ?

134.   Q.   What, secondly, did God do through His Son Jesus Christ?

135.   Q.   What, thirdly, did God do through His Son Jesus Christ?

136. Q. What, fourthly, did God do through His Son Jesus Christ?

137. Q. What, fifthly, did God do through his Son Jesus Christ?

138. Q. What, finally, does God propose to do through His Son Jesus Christ?

Lesson Thirty-Nine

THE ATONEMENT

Scripture Reading: Heb. 7:26-28, 9:11-28.

Scriptures to Memorize: "But Christ having come a high priest of the good things to come, through the greater and more perfect tabernacle, not made with hands, that is to say, not of this creation; nor yet through the blood of goats and calves, but through his own blood, entered in once for all into the holy place, having obtained eternal redemption" (Heb. 9:11-12). "For such a high priest became us, holy, guileless, undefiled, separated from sinners, and made higher than the heavens; who needeth not daily, like those high priests, to offer up sacrifices, first for his own sins, and then for the sins of the people: for this he did once for all, when he offered up himself" (Heb. 7:26-27).

139. Q. What was probably the most fundamental work that God wrought through His Son Jesus Christ?

A. The most fundamental work that God wrought through Christ, was the Atonement.

140. Q. What is meant by the Atonement?

A. By the Atonement is meant the Supreme Sacrifice of the Lamb of God Himself, offered by Himself acting in the capacity of our High Priest, for the sins of the world.

(1) 1 Cor. 15:3—"Christ died for our sins." Heb. 9:26—
"but now once at the end of the ages hath he been manifested to put away sin by the sacrifice of himself." John
1:29—"Behold, the Lamb of God, that taketh away the
sin of the world." Note how the sins of all humanity are,
in this text, bundled together and contemplated as a unit—
"the sin of the world." This means that the Lamb of God
Himself is the all-sufficient Atonement for all sin. (2)
"The Scriptures teach that Christ obeyed and suffered in
our stead, to satisfy an immanent demand of the Divine
Holiness, and thus remove an obstacle in the Divine Mind
to the pardon and restoration of the guilty" (A. H. Strong,
Systematic Theology, p. 713).

**141. Q. What is the first great truth involved in the
Atonement?**

**A. The truth that the Lamb of God is Himself our
all-sufficient Propitiation.**

It was never God's purpose to pass by any transgression of
His law without a just and adequate satisfaction. As Wat-
son says: "A government which admitted no forgiveness,
would sink the guilty to despair; a government which never
punishes offense, is a contradiction; it cannot exist. Not to
punish the guilty, is to dissolve authority; to punish without
mercy is to destroy, and where all are guilty, to make the
destruction universal." Hence, in view of the fact that
man was himself unable to provide an adequate atonement
for his sins, God provided it for him. The first object of
the incarnation and death of Christ was to meet and satisfy
the demands of Justice upon the sinner. Rom. 3:24, 25—
"Christ Jesus whom God set forth to be a propitiation,
through faith, in his blood." 1 John 2:1, 2—"Jesus Christ
the righteous . . . he is the propitiation for our sins." The
demands of Justice were met and satisfied more fully and
perfectly by Christ's offering of Himself for us, than if all
the penalties of violated law had been inflicted upon the
offending parties.

142. Q. What is the second great truth involved in the
           Atonement?

      A.   The truth that the Lamb of God is our all-suf-
           ficient Reconciliation.

Another object of the incarnation and death of Christ was
that God, by such a demonstration of His infinite love for
man, might furnish the incentives sufficient to change the
heart and disposition of the sinner and thus win him back
into covenant intimacy with Himself. The problem before
the Divine Government was not only that of satisfying the
claims of Justice, but also that of subduing and overcoming
the rebellion in man's heart. Obviously that could not have
been done by any infliction of punishment, because punishment would merely have increased the spirit of rebellion
and widened the breach. Hence the only course to pursue
to attain the end in view, was for God to make a demonstration of His amazing love and mercy, sufficient to overcome
the rebellion in the sinner's heart. To this end Christ gave
Himself freely for us all, that He might woo and win us
back to God. Eph. 2:15, 16—"that he might create in
himself of the two one new man, so making peace; and
might reconcile them both in one body unto God through
the cross." 2 Cor. 5:19—"God was in Christ reconciling
the world unto himself."

143. Q. What is the third great truth involved in the
           Atonement?

      A.   The truth that the Lamb of God is our suf-
           ficient Expiation.

Isa. 53:5—"He was wounded for our transgressions, he
was bruised for our iniquities; the chastisement of our peace
was upon him; and with his stripes we are healed." Heb.
9:26—"Now once at the end of the ages hath he been
manifested to put away sin by the sacrifice of himself."
1 John 3:5—"and ye know that he was manifested to take
away sins." Heb. 9:14—"how much more shall the blood

of Christ, who through the eternal Spirit offered himself without blemish unto God, cleanse your conscience from dead works to serve the living God?"

144. Q. What is the fourth great truth involved in the Atonement?

A. The truth that the Lamb of God is our all-sufficient Redemption.

His redemption is two fold, viz., the redemption of our spiritual nature from the bondage of sin (i. e., the guilt of sin), and the redemption of our fleshly nature from the bondage of death (i. e., the consequences of sin). This redemption includes also redemption from deformity. There will be no cripples in Heaven. Rom. 3:24—"being justified freely by his grace through the redemption that is in Christ Jesus." Gal. 3:13—"Christ redeemed us from the curse of the law." 1 Cor. 6:19, 20—"ye are not your own; for ye were bought with a price: glorify God therefore in your body." Acts 20:28—"to feed the church of the Lord which he purchased with his own blood." Rom. 8:23—"even we ourselves groan within ourselves, waiting for our adoption, to wit, the redemption of our body." Cf. Heb. 2:14, 15; 1 John 3:3; 1 Cor. 15:25-26; Phil. 3:20-21; Rom. 8:11; Rev. 20:10, 14; 1 Cor. 15:35-57.

145. Q. Did Jesus die for us because He was under obligation of any kind to have done so?

A. No. He gave Himself voluntarily, willingly, and freely, for our sins.

1 Cor. 15:3—"Christ died for our sins." Gal. 1:3, 4—"our Lord Jesus Christ, who gave himself for our sins." 1 Pet. 2:24—"who his own self bare our sins in his body upon the tree." Rom. 5:8—"while we were yet sinners, Christ died for us." Tit. 3:13, 14—"Jesus Christ who gave himself for us, that he might redeem us from all iniquity." Eph. 5:25—"even as Christ also loved the church, and gave himself up for it." God gave His Son, and the Son

gave His life, not because either was under obligation to have done so, but because both Father and Son loved us too much to allow us to perish forever, without the opportunities and means of salvation.

146. Q. Are the provisions and benefits of Christ's death for all men, unconditionally?

A. No. They are for those only, who accept and appropriate them by faith.

(1) Rev. 22:17—"he that will, let him take the water of life freely." John 10:10—"I am come that they may have life, and may have it abundantly." John 5:40—"ye will not come to me, that ye may have life." Llke 13:3—"Except ye repent, ye shall all in like manner perish." Heb. 5:9—"having been made perfect (i. e., through suffering), he became unto all them that obey him the author of eternal salvation." (2) While the Sacrifice which Christ provided is as universal as sin in its scope, the sins only of the obedient are expiated by it. "Its design, then, is necessarily limited to all who come to God by it; while its value and efficacy are equal to the salvation of the whole world, provided only they will put themselves under the covering of its propitiatory power" (Campbell, **Christian System,** p. 43). (See Question 46.)

147. Q. What, then, is the most fundamental fact of all time and eternity?

A. The most fundamental fact of all time and eternity is the Atonement.

(1) It is the only Sacrifice for sin—the all-sufficient and final demonstration to the world of God's love and mercy. All the animal sacrifices of preceding dispensations were related to it only as substitutes and types. Christ, we are told, officiated as our High Priest "once for all, when he offered up himself" (Heb. 7:27). He was "once offered to bear the sins of many" (Heb. 9:28). "Now once at the end of the ages hath he been manifested to put away sin

by the sacrifice of himself" (Heb. 9:26). He "suffered for sins once, the righteous for the unrighteous, that he might bring us to God" (1 Pet. 3:18). "For the death that he died, he died unto sin once" (Rom. 6:10); and having thus "offered one sacrifice for sins for ever, sat down on the right hand of God" (Heb. 10:12). (2) We are told, furthermore, that all through the coming ages the moral splendors of God's character and work are to find their most vivid illustration in the works and wonders of re' demption; "that in the ages to come he might show the exceeding riches of his grace in kindness toward us in Christ Jesus" (Eph. 3:7). (3) Finally, in order that we may un' derstand, even though imperfectly, how closely related the Atonement stands to the whole moral universe, we need only read that it was God's eternal purpose "unto a dispen' sation of the fulness of the times, to sum up all things in Christ, the things in the heavens, and the things upon the earth" (Eph. 1:10). "For he must reign, till he hath put all enemies under his feet" (1 Cor. 15:25). "Wherefore also God highly exalted him, and gave unto him the name which is above every name; that in the name of Jesus every knee should bow, of things in heaven and things on earth and things under the earth, and that every tongue should confess that Jesus Christ is Lord, to the glory of God the Father" (Phil. 3:9-10). It will thus be seen that the Atone' ment is central, in the moral universe, in revelation, in re' demption, in this world, and in the ages to come.

148.   Q.   What tragic implication is involved in the no-
                tion that the death of Jesus was only a martyr-
                dom?

         A.   If the death of Jesus was a martyrdom and
                nothing more, it follows that mankind is still
                without an Atonement and consequently hope-
                lessly lost in sin.

(1) If the death of Jesus was merely that of a human being,

it had no more efficacy in satisfying the demands of Justice upon a sinful race, than the death of Socrates, or Abraham Lincoln, or of any other man who has given his life for the betterment of the race, would have. (2) If Jesus died merely as a martyr, and not as the Atonement for the sins of the world, then the whole human race is back where it was two thousand years ago, floundering in the mire of Natural Religion and Philosophy. (3) The death of Jesus was a Perfect Sacrifice for sin, because He was the Word who became flesh and dwelt among us (John 1:14); because He was divine as well as human, God as well as man, the God-man, the Divine-human Person (Matt. 1:23), the One who "hath been in all points tempted like as we are, yet without sin" (Heb. 4:15), the One who was "holy, guileless, undefiled, separated from sinners, and made higher than the heavens" (Heb. 9:26). The Divine nature which He offered up was self-existent and holy. The human nature which He offered up was equally unstained by human corruption and depravity. Therefore in giving Himself He offered up a Divine gift which was amply sufficient to satisfy the demands of Justice with regard to the transgression of Divine law. In short, His was the Perfect Atonement for sin; and so we sing, with Isaac Watts:

"Forbid it, Lord, that I should boast,
   Save in the death of Christ, my God;
All the vain things that charm me most,
   I sacrifice them to His blood.
"Were the whole realm of nature mine,
   That were a present far too small;
Love so amazing, so divine,
   Demands my soul, my life, my all."

149. Q. What, then, is our Altar under the Christian Dispensation?

A. Our Altar is Calvary.

150. Q. What is our Sacrifice?

A. Our Sacrifice is Christ who, as our High Priest, offered Himself, as the Lamb of God, for the sins of the world.

151. Q. Who is our High Priest under the Christian Dispensation?

A. Christ Himself.

Heb. 7:17—"Thou art a priest for ever, after the order of Melchizedek" (Psa. 110:4); that is, like Melchizedek who was both "king of Salem" and "priest of God Most High" (Gen. 17-18), Christ is our High Priest and also our King. 1 Tim. 1:17—"Now unto the King eternal." 1 Tim. 6:15, Rev. 17:14, 19:16—"the King of kings, and Lord of lords." See also Heb. 7:26-27, 9:11-12.

152. Q. What is our Priesthood under the Christian Dispensation?

A. It is a priesthood of all believers.

1 Pet. 2:5—"ye also, as living stones, are built up a spiritual house, to be a holy priesthood, to offer up spiritual sacrifices, acceptable to God through Jesus Christ." 1 Pet. 2:9 —"ye are an elect race, a royal priesthood," etc. Rev. 1:5, 6—"Unto him that loveth us, and loosed us from our sins by his blood; and he made us to be a kingdom, to be priests unto his God and Father." Cf. Rev. 5:10, 20:6. Rom. 12:1—"I beseech you, therefore, brethren, by the mercies of God, to present your bodies a living sacrifice, holy, acceptable to God, which is your spiritual service." Heb. 13:15—"through him then let us offer up a sacrifice of praise continually, that is, the fruit of lips which make confession to his name."

153. Q. Is there any authority in the New Testament for a special human priesthood under the Christian Dispensation?

A. There is not.

There is neither command nor precedent for a special order

of priests under the Covenant of Grace. Jesus says: "Call no man your father on the earth; for one is your Father, even he who is in heaven" (Matt. 23:9).

154. Q. **What is our privilege as priests unto God?**

A. **It is our privilege, and should be our greatest joy, to offer up to God spiritual sacrifices of prayer, praise, thanksgiving, devotion and service.**

The following chart will serve as a summarization of the development of true religion through the ages:

Dispensation	Altar	Sacrifice	Priesthood
Patriarchal	Family Altar	Animal Sacrifice	Patriarchal Prieshood
Jewish	National Altar	Animal Sacrifice	Levitical Prieshood
Christian	Calvary—the Universal Altar	The Lamb of God	The Priesthood of all Believers

REVIEW EXAMINATION OVER LESSON THIRTY-NINE

139. Q. What was probably the most fundamental work that God wrought through His Son Jesus Christ?

140. Q. What is meant by the Atonement?

141. Q. What is the first great truth involved in the Atonement?

142. Q. What is the second great truth involved in the Atonement?

143. Q. What is the third great truth involved in the Atonement?

144. Q. What is the fourth great truth involved in the Atonement?

145. Q. Did Jesus die for us because He was under obligation of any kind to have done so?

146. Q. Are the provisions and benefits of Christ's death for all men, unconditionally?

147. Q. What, then, is the most fundamental fact of all time and eternity?

148. Q. What tragic implication is involved in the notion that the death of Jesus was only a martyrdom?

149. Q. What, then, is our Altar under the Christian Dispensation?

150. Q. What is our Sacrifice?

151. Q. Who is our High Priest under the Christian Dispensation?

152. Q. What is our Priesthood under the Christian Dispensation?

153. Q. Is there any authority in the New Testament for a special human priesthood under the Christian Dispensation?

154. Q. What is our privilege as priests unto God?

SPECIAL STUDY: ON THE WORD "RELIGION"

A few remarks are in order here about the etymology of the word, "religion."

Cicero (De Natura Deorum, 2, 28, 72) derives it from the Latin third-conjugation verb relego, relegere, meaning "to go over again," that is, in reading, in speech, or in thought, "to consider carefully," and hence, as used by him—Cicero —to mean "reverent observance" (of duties to the gods). Although this may have been the pagan notion of the word, certainly it is not the Biblical meaning of it.

According to Lactantius (Divina Instituta, 4, 28) and Augustine (Retractiones, 1, 13), "religion" derives from the first-conjugation Latin verb, religo, religare, meaning "to bind back," "to bind anew," etc. Harper's Latin Dictionary (Andrews' Freund, revised by Lewis and Short) has this to say (s.v.): "Modern etymologists mostly agree with this latter view, assuming as root, **lig**, to bind, whence also **lictor, lex,** and **ligare**; hence, **religio** sometimes means the same as **obligatio**." The close relationship of the family of words formed around the root **lig** (ligament, ligature, oblige, etc.) to that formed around the root **leg (lex, legis, "law," legislate, legal, etc.)** is too obvious to be ignored. These two families of words both have the connotation of a binding force. Whatever the word "religion" may have meant to the pagan world, the fact remains that the essence of Biblical religion is **a binding of a person anew to God** (healing of the schism caused by sin: the God of the Bible is the covenant God), and is fully expressed in the word "reconciliation" (2 Cor. 5:17-21). As a consequence of this healing through regeneration and continuous sanctification, the righteous person ultimately attains **holiness** (from **holon,** "whole), which is wholeness or perfection (that is, completeness, from **per** plus **facere,** "to make thorough, complete"). Matt. 5:48—"Ye therefore shall be perfect, as your heavenly Father is perfect." The attainment of this perfection is consummated, of course, in the ultimate redemption of the body (Rom. 8:18-24, 8:11; 1 Cor. 15:35-58; 2 Cor. 5:1-10; Phil. 3:20-21, etc.).

SPECIAL STUDY: ON THE DISPENSATIONS

Also, it will be noted that in Lesson Twenty-Nine of this section, I have referred to the Patriarchal, Jewish, and Christian systems as three revealed "religions." Strictly speaking, however, according to the teaching of the Bible itself, these are three successive Dispensations of the one progressive revelation of true religion. The Dispensations changed — from the family to the national to the universal — as the type of priesthood changed. The Patriarchal Dispensation was the age of family rule and family worship, with the patriarch (paternal head) acting as prophet (revealer of God's will), priest (intercessor) and king for his entire progeny. The Jewish Dispensation was ushered in with the establishment of a national institution of worship (the Tabernacle, and later the Temple) and a national priesthood (the Levitical or Aaronic priesthood). The Christian Dispensation had its beginning with the abroga-tion of the Old Covenant and the ratification of the New by one and the same event—the death of Christ on the Cross (although the Jewish Institution was permitted to remain as a social and civil institution some forty years longer, that is, down to the destruction of Jerusalem and the dispersion of its people by the Roman armies, A.D. 70). (Cf. Jn. 1:17, Gal. 3:23-29, 2 Cor. 3:1-11, Col. 2:13-15, and especially the seventh, eighth, ninth, and tenth chap-ters of the Epistle to the Hebrews.) Under the Christian System all Christians are priests unto God, and Christ is their High Priest (1 Pet. 2:5, 9; Rev. 5:10; Rom. 12:1-2, 8:34; Heb. 2:17, also chs. 3, 5, 7; 1 Tim. 2:5, 1 Jn. 2:1, etc.). It will be recalled that Alexander Campbell referred to the Patriarchal Dispensation as the starlight age, to the Jewish Dispensation as the moonlight age, to the special ministry of John the Baptizer (to the Jewish nation) as the twilight age, and to the present or Christian Dispensation (which may also rightly be designated the Dispensation of the Holy Spirit) as the sunlight age, of the unfolding of the divine Plan of Redemption. These successive "ages," therefore, embrace the successive stages in the revelation of true religion as set forth in the Bible. Refusal to recognize this fundamental unity of the Bible as a whole can result only in confusion, presumption, and ultimate rejection by the Author of the Bible Himself.

It will be noted also that Christ Himself is both Sacrifice and Priest in the present Dispensation. In the diagram fol-lowing Lesson 39 herein, I have suggested that our uni-versal Altar in this Dispensation was Calvary or the Cross. I am not unmindful of the fact that there are Bible scholars who insist that our Lord's perfect human nature was itself the Altar upon which He, as the Lamb of God who "taketh away the sin of the world" (Jn. 1:29) offered up His divine nature as the perfect Sacrifice (Atonement or Covering) for human sin. I consider this point well taken. (Cf. Heb. 10:5, 2:14; 1 Pet. 2:24; Heb. 4:14-16; Luke 1:26-28, etc.) Does not Luke's language here mean that the Holy Spirit created the physical nature of Jesus in the womb of the virgin? That is to say, as the Spirit brooded over the primeval chaos "in the beginning," to initiate the physical or cosmic creation, so did the same Spirit brood over ("overshadow") the womb of the virgin Mary thus to initiate the new creation (re-creation). (Cf. Gen. 1:2, Gal. 4:4, Luke 1:35, etc.) The handiwork of this last brooding was the perfect human nature of God's Only Begotten, the human nature that was designed to serve as the perfect Altar for His Atoning Sacrifice of His divine nature (Jn. 1:1-3, 1:14). Nor does this mean that He was any the less human because of this divine "overshadowing" (Matt. 1:23). On the contrary, is not sin always more painful, more tragic, more repulsive, to Perfection — Holiness — than it could ever be to us ordinary mortals? Cf. Luke 22:44, Heb. 5:7, Matt. 27:46, Isa. 63:3. This perfect body which was of the Spirit's begetting was by this fact qualitatively prepared to be the perfect Atonement for sin, and so constituted that death had no power over it (Ps. 16:8-10; Acts 2:24-32, 13: 35-37). Thus do the basic doctrines of the Christian faith — the Virgin Birth, the Atonement, and the Resurrection — all combine in the divine plan to which each contributes its indispensable part: to reject one of these doctrines is to reject them all.

Finally, this divine begetting of the physical nature of God's Only Begotten makes clear the reason for God's law respecting the constituent elements of the sacrificial altars of the Patriarchal and Jewish Dispensations, namely, that these altars were to be constructed of "unhewn" (that is, natural) stones (no tool was to be used upon them, Exo. 20:24-25, Deut. 27:5-6). Thus did the altars of olden times serve as types of the Universal Altar (Christ's perfect human nature), just as the sacrificial lambs offered upon them served as types of the Lamb of God, our Passover (1 Cor. 5:7).

To summarize: in the Christian Dispensation, Christ Jesus is our Altar, our Sacrifice, and our one and only Priest (King-Priest after the order of Melchizedek, Ps. 110:4; Heb. 6:20, 7:1-25). It was the Mystery of God's Will, according to His good pleasure, which He purposed in Christ "unto a dispensation of the fulness of the times, to sum up all things in Christ, the things in the heavens, and the things upon the earth; in him, I say, in whom also we were made a heritage, having been foreordained according to the purpose of him who worketh all things after the counsel of his will," etc. (Eph. 1:9-12).

Lesson Forty
THE NEW COVENANT

Scripture Reading: Heb. 8; 2 Cor. 3.

Scriptures to Memorize: "For the law was given through Moses; grace and truth came through Jesus Christ" (John 1:17). "So that the law is become our tutor to bring us unto Christ, that we might be justified by faith. But now that faith is come, we are no longer under a tutor" Gal. 3: 24-25). "But now hath he obtained a ministry the more excellent, by so much as he is also the mediator of a better covenant, which hath been enacted upon better promises" (Heb. 8:6).

1. Q. What was the first step in the unfolding of God's Plan of Redemption for man?

A. The first step was the Divine announcement that redemption would be provided for man, through the Seed of a woman.

The mysterious oracle in which this Divine announcement was included, was spoken by Jehovah Himself, immediately after the fall of our first parents. (See Lesson Twenty-Seven, Questions 4-6 inclusive.) Gen. 3:14-15.

2. Q. What was the second step in the unfolding of God's Plan of Redemption for man?

A. The second step was the giving of the Abrahamic Promise and the inauguration of the Old Covenant with Abraham and his posterity.

Gen. 12:1-4, 13:14-18, 15:3-5, 17:1-14, 22:9-19; Gal. 3:7-9, 3:16, 3:23-29, etc. (See Lesson Thirty-Two, Questions 74-80 inclusive.)

3. Q. What was the third step in the unfolding of God's Plan of Redemption for man?

A. The third step was the establishment of the Mosaic System to prepare the way for and point forward to, in type, symbol and prophecy, the events, institutions and laws of the Christian System.

The Abrahamic covenant was enlarged into a national covenant at Sinai, through the mediatorship of Moses. At the same time the Law was given, in which the eternal principles of right and wrong were established. This entire Old Covenant was for the purpose of preparing the way for, and proving the divine origin of, the New Covenant and its institutions. (See Lessons Thirty-Three-Thirty-Five inclusive.)

4. Q. What was the fourth step in the unfolding of God's Plan of Redemption for man?

A. The fourth step was the raising up of the Hebrew prophets to foretell the details of the life, work and reign of the Messiah.

This body of Old Testament prophecy was for the purpose of identifying the true Messiah at His coming. The Messianic predictions of the Old Testament were all fulfilled in the life and ministry of Jesus. (See Lesson Thirty-Six.)

5. Q. **What was the fifth step in the unfolding of God's Plan of Redemption for man?**

A. **The fifth step was the ministry of John the Baptizer.**

(See Lesson Thirty-Seven, Questions 124-125.)

6. Q. **What was the special work of John the Baptizer?**

A. **It was to herald the advent and reign of the Messiah.**

John was the forerunner of the Christ. (The title Christ means The Anointed One.) See Isa. 40:3, Matt. 3:3, Luke 3:4-6, John 1:23. Cf. Luke 1:76—"Thou shalt go before the face of the Lord to make ready his ways."

7. Q. **What was the sixth step in the unfolding of God's Plan of Redemption for man?**

A. **The sixth step was the ministry of the Incarnate Word.**

(1) The Incarnate Word, i. e., the Word who became flesh and dwelt among us (John 1:14), was Jesus of Nazareth, the Christ, the Son of the living God. It was He who executed God's Plan of Redemption for us. (2) This phase of the unfolding of God's plan included: the entrance of the Word into human flesh; His work and ministry as the Revealer of God and our Perfect Exemplar; His death on the Cross as the all-sufficient Atonement for the sins of the world; His death, burial and resurrection; His ascension to the right hand of the Father; and His coronation as King of kings and Lord of lords. (See Lessons Thirty-Eight and Thirty-Nine.)

8. Q. **What was the connection between the personal ministry of Jesus and the Jewish nation?**

A. **The personal ministry of Jesus was a special dispensation of God's grace towards the Jewish nation.**

(1) John 1:11—"He came unto His own, and they that were his own received him not." His own people rejected Him, and their ecclesiastical leaders coerced the Roman officials into executing the death sentence. The rabble shouted: "His blood be on us, and on our children" (Matt. 27:25). (2) The personal ministry of Jesus was under the Mosaic Law, to which He rendered a faultless obedience. Matt. 5:17—"Think not that I came to destroy the law or the prophets: I came not to destroy, but to fulfill." Jesus fulfilled the Mosaic Code in the sense that He obeyed its requirements perfectly. (3) The First Commission was: "Go not into any way of the Gentiles, and enter not into any city of the Samaritans: but go rather to the lost sheep of the house of Israel" (Matt. 10:5, 6). It was not until after His death, burial and resurrection, that He gave the last and Great Commission; in which He authorized His evangelists to go into all the world (Mark 16:15) and make disciples of all the nations (Matt. 28:19).

9. Q. **When did the present or Christian Dispensation begin?**

   A. **It began with the ratification of the New Covenant by the death of Christ.**

10. Q. **What is the New Covenant?**

    A. **It is the Covenant of Grace mediated by Jesus Christ.**

(1) In scripture, a covenant is a solemn religious compact or agreement. "The Greeks had two words for **covenant,** viz., **syntheke,** and **diatheke.** The former was used to denote a solemn agreement made between equals; and the latter, to denote any arrangement made by a superior for the acceptance of an inferior. And hence it is, that all of God's covenants are expressed in Greek by the word

diatheke" (Milligan, **Scheme of Redemption,** p. 77, fn.).
(2) Three factors enter into the making of every covenant,
viz., the covenanter, the covenantee, and the stipulations
agreed upon. (3) The Bible is the history of two great
Covenants. The first or Old Covenant, the Covenant of
Law (otherwise known as "the letter," "the ministration
of death," "the ministration of condemnation," etc.) was
made with the Hebrew people through the mediatorship of
Moses. The last or New Covenant, the Covenant of Grace,
the Gospel Covenant (otherwise known as "the spirit,"
"the ministration of the spirit," "the ministration of right'
eousness," etc.) is entered into, with all obedient believers,
through the mediation of Jesus Christ. See Jer. 31:31-34;
John 1:17; 2 Cor. 3:1-11; Heb. 8; Gal. 3:24-29; Col. 2:13-
15, etc.

11. Q. **What was the final step in the unfolding of
God's Plan of Redemption for man?**

A. **The final step was the inauguration of the Christian System, its principles, laws and institutions.**
This last phase of the unfolding of God's plan included: (1)
the giving of the Great Commission; (2) the descent of
the Holy Spirit to act as the Agent of the God-head upon
earth during the present Dispensation; (3) the proclamation
of the facts, commands and promises of the Gospel; (4)
the incorporation of the Church of Christ; (5) the estab'
lishment of the Christian ordinances and Christian worship;
(6) the writing and compiling of the New Testament Scrip'
tures to serve as an all-sufficient guide in religious faith and
practice for the true Church until Jesus comes again.

12. Q. **For what should we who live in the present Dispensation be especially thankful?**

A. **We should be especially thankful that we are
under the provisions of the New Covenant
"which hath been enacted upon better promises"
(Heb. 8:6)**

The Old Covenant was ritualistic, legal, ceremonial; the New is essentially spiritual. The basis of membership in the Old was fleshly; the basis of membership in the New is spiritual. John 3:3—"Except one be born anew, he can-not see the kingdom of God." The Old was the "ministra-tion of death," in the sense that the penalty for its viola-tion was usually capital punishment (stoning to death); and the "ministration of condemnation," in the sense that the tendency of the Law was to identify sin and thus con-demn the sinner (2 Cor. 3:7, 9). The New is the "minis-tration of the spirit" in the sense it is spiritual in its essen-tial nature; and "the ministration of righteousness" in the sense that it is primarily designed to nurture faith and holi-ness in the individual (2 Cor. 3:8, 9). In addition to all this, the New "hath been enacted upon better promises," viz., remission of sins, the indwelling of the Holy Spirit, and eternal life (Acts 2:38, Rom. 6:23). Let us therefore thank God that we are living under the provisions, privi-leges and blessings of the New Covenant!

REVIEW EXAMINATION OVER LESSON FORTY

1. Q.   What was the first step in the unfolding of God's Plan of Redemption for man?

2. Q.   What was the second step in the unfolding of God's Plan of Redemption for man?

3. Q.   What was the third step in the unfolding of God's Plan of Redemption for man?

4. Q.   What was the fourth step in the unfolding of God's Plan of Redemption for man?

5. Q.   What was the fifth step in the unfolding of God's Plan of Redemption for man?

6. Q.   What was the special work of John the Baptizer?

7. Q.   What was the sixth step in the unfolding of God's Plan of Redemption for man?

8. Q.   What was the connection between the personal ministry of Jesus and the Jewish nation?

9. Q. When did the present or Christian Dispensation begin?
10. Q. What is the New Covenant?
11. Q. What was the final step in the unfolding of God's Plan of Redemption for man?
12. Q. For what should we who live in the present Dispensation be especially thankful?

Lesson Forty-One
WHAT GOD DID THROUGH THE APOSTLES

Scripture Reading: Acts 1:1-8, 2 Cor. 5:16-20.

Scriptures to Memorize: "But ye shall receive power, when the Holy Spirit is come upon you; and ye shall be my witnesses both in Jerusalem, and in all Judea and Samaria, and unto the uttermost part of the earth" (Acts 1:8). "We are ambassadors therefore on behalf of Christ, as though God were entreating by us; we beseech you on behalf of Christ, be ye reconciled to God" (2 Cor. 5:20).

13. Q. What do we mean by the New Testament?
    A. By the New Testament, we mean the Last Will and Testament of our Lord and Savior Jesus Christ.

(1) The word covenant is, in the Latin, **testamentum**, rendered in our language, testament. A testament is, in ordinary terms, a will. A will is defined as "a legal document disposing of one's property at death." (2) Hence the New Testament is the formal and authoritative instrument through which Jesus Christ, the Testator, at His death, authorized the continued disposition to men, on the terms specified therein, of the blessings and gifts of Divine grace, throughout the present or Christian Dispensation. (3) The Christian System is spoken of as a covenant, in the sense that it is a solemn proposal from God, through Christ, ad-

dressed to sinful men, inviting them to turn again (conver' sion) and enter into a spiritual compact with their heaven' ly Father and their Redeemer; and stating the terms upon which such solemn agreement may be consummated. (4) The Christian System is spoken of as a Testament, in the sense that it is the final and authoritative revelation of the will of God, through Jesus Christ, respecting the means and provisions for man's eternal redemption. This Last Will and Testament is recorded in that portion of the Bible which we know as the New Testament Scriptures.

14. Q. What are the essential elements of a testament or will?

A. They are: (1) the will-maker, or testator; (2) the stipulations; and (3) the executor or executors.

15. Q. When did the Last Will and Testament of our Lord and Savior Jesus Christ go into effect?

A. It went into effect at the death of Christ.

A will becomes effective as soon as the will-maker dies. Hence the New Testament went into effect when Christ died on the Cross. Heb. 9:16—"For where a testament is, there must of necessity be the death of him that made it."

16. Q. What was the first necessary step in the execu' tion of the Last Will and Testament of our Lord and Savior Jesus Christ?

A. The first necessary step was the probating of the instrument.

The first necessary step in the execution of any will is the certification of its authenticity in open court. This step is known as the probating of the will.

17. Q. When was the Last Will and Testament of our Lord and Savior Jesus Christ probated?

A. It was probated on the first Pentecost after the resurrection of Christ, A. D. 30.

On that memorable day, the terms and conditions of the New Testament (i. e., the facts, commands and promises of the Gospel Covenant) were publicly announced for the first time. They were announced by the Apostles as the divinely-appointed executors; and they were properly authenticated by the Holy Spirit sent down from heaven. (See the entire second chapter of Acts; cf. 1 Pet. 1:12.)

18. Q. **Who were the executors of the Last Will and Testament of our Lord and Savior Jesus Christ?**

A. **The Apostles.**

An executor is "a person appointed by a testator in his will to see that the terms of the will are duly carried out." Our Lord appointed the Apostles the executors of His Last Will and Testament. Matt. 18:18—"What things soever ye shall loose on earth shall be loosed in heaven." John 20:21-23, "Jesus therefore said to them again, Peace be unto you: as the Father hath sent me, even so I send you. And when he had said this, he breathed on them, and saith unto them, Receive ye the Holy Spirit; whose soever sins ye forgive, they are forgiven unto them; whose soever sins ye retain, they are retained." John 17:18—"As thou didst send me into the world, even so sent I them into the world." These scriptures all have reference to the Apostles only. Cf. Acts 1:1-8.

19. Q. **Who, then, were the Apostles?**

A. **The Apostles were men specially called, trained and qualified by Christ Himself, for the work of executing His Last Will and Testament.**

(1) They were men whom Jesus Himself called. Matt. 4:18-21, 9:9, 10:2-4; Mark 1:16-19, 3:13-19; Luke 5:10, 6:13-16; John 1:35-51, etc. His personal appearance to Saul of Tarsus was for the purpose of calling the latter to the apostleship. Acts 26:15-18. (2) They were men whom Jesus Himself personally trained and qualified for their work. See Acts 1:21-22; John 17:7-16; 1 Cor. 13:37,

etc. (3) They were men who actually saw the Lord after His resurrection. See Acts 10:40-41; 1 John 1:1-4; Acts 9:1-9, 26:12-18, etc.

20. Q. Name the original Twelve Apostles.

A. They were: (1) Simon Peter; (2) Andrew; (3) James, and (4) John, the sons of Zebedee; (5) Philip; (6) Bartholomew (Nathanael); (7) Matthew (Levi); (8) Thomas; (9) James the son of Alpheus; (10) Judas (also Thaddeus, or Jude); (11) Simon Zelotes (the Cananean); and (12) Judas Iscariot.

Of this original group Judas Iscariot betrayed Christ and fell from the apostleship. Later, Matthias was selected to take his place. See Acts 1:15-26. That the selection of Matthias was divinely ratified, is evident from a comparison of Acts 1:26 with Acts 6:2. Acts 1:26—"the lot fell upon Matthias, and he was numbered with the **eleven** apostles." Acts 6:2—"and the **twelve** called the multitude of the disciples unto them," etc.

21. Q. Who was specially called, trained and qualified to be the Apostle to the Gentiles?

A. Paul.

Saul was his Hebrew name, but he was also born a Roman citizen and bore the additional name of Paul. See Acts 26:12-19; Gal. 1:11-12; 1 Cor. 9:1; 1 Cor. 14:37, etc.

22. Q. What is the term most commonly applied to the Apostles in the New Testament Scriptures?

A. They are alluded to most frequently as "witnesses."

Acts 1:8—"ye shall be my witnesses." Acts 2:32—"This Jesus did God raise up, whereof we are all witnesses." Acts 10:40-41—"Him God raised up the third day, and gave him to be made manifest, not to all the people, but unto witnesses that were chosen before of God, even to us, who ate and drank with him after he rose from the dead." Luke 24:48—"Ye are witnesses of these things." Jesus, in commissioning Paul, said: "to this end have I appeared unto thee, to appoint thee a minister and a witness both of the things wherein thou hast seen me, and of the things wherein I will appear unto thee" (Acts 26:16). Cf. also Acts 1:22, 1 Cor. 9:1, 2 Pet. 1:16-18, 1 John 1:1-4, etc.

23.   Q.   What is the signification of the term "witness"?

A.   It signifies authenticity.

(1) A witness is one who testifies; one who testifies with regard to what he has seen, with his own eyes; and one whose testimony is therefore authentic. (2) The Apostles were not priests; nor were they theologians, philosophers, clergymen, or social reformers. They were primarily and essentially witnesses. They were men who testified with regard to what they had actually seen. Acts 10:41—"to us, who ate and drank with him after he rose from the dead." 1 John 1:1—"that which we have seen with our eyes, that which we beheld, and our hands handled," etc. We are therefore justified in accepting the testimony of the Apostles as authentic.

24.   Q.   Where is the apostolic testimony recorded?

A.   It is recorded in the New Testament Scriptures.

In and through the New Testament Scriptures, the Apostles have literally become witnesses of Christ unto the uttermost parts of the earth (Acts 1:8). We, as disciples, evangelists, elders, deacons, teachers, etc., cannot be witnesses of Christ; rather, we are the propagators and preachers of the apostolic witness or testimony. 2 Tim. 2:2—"and the things which thou hast heard from me among many witnesses, the same commit thou to faithful men, who shall be able to teach others also."

25.   Q.   What other special designation is given to the Apostles in the New Testament Scriptures?

A. They are called "ambassadors" of Christ.

2 Cor. 5:20—"we are ambassadors therefore on behalf of Christ." Eph. 6:19-20—"the mystery of the gospel, for which I am an ambassador in chains."

26. Q. What is the signification of the term "ambassador"?

A. It signifies authority.

(1) An ambassador is a government agent of highest rank. Hence the term "ambassador" is the only one that can be used to appropriately describe the dignity and rank of the apostolic office. (2) An ambassador is always vested with the authority of the government which he is sent out to represent. The Apostles were ambassadors of Christ, there-fore, in the sense that they were sent out fully clothed with His divine authority. John 17:18—"As thou didst send me into the world, even so sent I them into the world." John 20:21, 23—"as the Father hath sent me, even so send I you . . . whose soever sins ye forgive, they are forgiven unto them; whose soever sins ye retain, they are retained." Mark 16:20—"And they went forth, and preached every-where, the Lord working with them, and confirming the word by the signs that followed."

27. Q. How were the Apostles specially qualified for the work they were sent out to do?

A. They were specially qualified by having been given the Holy Spirit to accompany them, to direct them in their work, and to guide them into all the truth.

Note the many promises that were made to the Apostles, and to the Apostles only. Matt. 10:19-20—"It shall be given you in that hour what ye shall speak. For it is not ye that speak, but the Spirit of your Father that speaketh in you." John 14:26—"But the Comforter, even the Holy Spirit, whom the Father will send in my name, he shall teach you all things, and bring to your remembrance all that I said unto you." Luke 24:48, 49—"Ye are witnesses of these things ... but tarry ye in the city until ye be clothed with power from on high." Acts 1:8—"But ye shall receive power, when the Holy Spirit is come upon you; and ye shall be my witnesses," etc. Cf. John 14:16-17, 15:26-27, 16:7-15, 20:21-23, etc. Acts 2:4—"And they were all filled with the Holy Spirit, and began to speak with other tongues, as the Spirit gave them utterance." It should be made clear that these promises were to the Apostles only, not to all Christians. To interpret them as having reference to all believers, as is frequently done, is to give them a wholly unscriptural implication.

28.   Q.   For what purpose were the gifts and powers of the Holy Spirit bestowed upon the Apostles in such great measure?

A.   For the purpose of making them infallible witnesses.

This guidance and inspiration of the Holy Spirit was for the purpose of clothing them with infallibility. They were thus safeguarded against error in executing the Last Will and Testament of our Lord and Savior Jesus Christ. John 16:13—"Howbeit when he, the Spirit of truth, is come, he shall guide you into all the truth ... and he shall declare unto you the things that are to come." Cf. 1 Cor. 2:12, 13; 1 Pet. 1:12; 1 Thess. 2:13; 1 Cor. 14:37; Acts 15:28, etc.

29.   Q.   Did the Apostles have any successors?

A.   They did not; for the obvious reason that witnesses cannot have successors.

A witness can testify only with regard to what he himself has seen, with his own eyes; hence a witness cannot have successors. There is not one iota of evidence in the New Testament Scriptures, either by direct statement or by inference, that the Apostles called or qualified, or delegated their authority to, any man or group of men to succeed them. With the establishment of the Church, and the writing of the New Testament Scriptures, the office and work of the Apostles came to an end. The dogma of "apostolic succession" is a monstrous fabrication of purely human origin, and without any divine warrant whatsoever.

30. Q. What, firstly, did God do through the Apostles?

A. Through the Apostles, He revealed and established the principles, laws and institutions of the New Covenant.

31. Q. What, secondly, did God do through the Apostles?

A. Through the Apostles, He gave the Great Commission under which the Church functions in evangelizing the world.

Acts 1:2—"until the day in which he was received up, after that he had given commandment through the Holy Spirit unto the apostles whom he had chosen." This "commandment" is generally known as the Great Commission—"the marching orders of the King." Matt. 28:19-20, "Go ye therefore, and make disciples of all the nations, baptizing them into the name of the Father and of the Son and of the Holy Spirit: teaching them to observe all things whatsoever I commanded you: and lo, I am with you always, even unto the end of the world." Mark 16:15, 16—"Go ye into all the world and preach the gospel to the whole creation. He that believeth and is baptized shall be saved; but he that disbelieveth shall be condemned."

32. Q. What, thirdly, did God do through the Apostles?

A. Through the Apostles, He set up the Church of Christ to preserve and proclaim the Gospel for a testimony unto all the nations (Matt. 24:14).

33. Q. What, fourthly, did God do through the Apostles?

A. Through the Apostles, He embodied the Christian Revelation in permanent form in the New

Testament Scriptures, for the guidance of His people under the New Covenant.

The Apostles' teaching, as embodied in the New Testament Scriptures, is for the administration of the Church throughout the Christian Dispensation. We read that the church at Jerusalem "continued stedfastly in the apostles' teaching" (Acts 2:42); so should all Christians. The New Testament canon is our all-sufficient guide in religious faith, worship and practice. It is the only Discipline we need. Let us therefore plead with believers everywhere to abandon all divisive and unscriptural creeds and confessions, which have been written by men; and to adhere solely to the teaching of the New Testament Scriptures.

REVIEW EXAMINATION OVER LESSON FORTY-ONE

13. Q. What do we mean by the New Testament?
14. Q. What are the essential elements of a testament or will?
15. Q. When did the Last Will and Testament of our Lord and Savior Jesus Christ go into effect?
16. Q. What was the first necessary step in the execution of the Last Will and Testament of our Lord and Savior Jesus Christ?
17. Q. When was the Last Will and Testament of our Lord and Savior Jesus Christ probated?
18. Q. Who were the executors of the Last Will and Testament of our Lord and Savior Jesus Christ?
19. Q. Who, then, were the Apostles?
20. Q. Name the original Twelve Apostles.
21. Q. Who was specially called, trained and qualified to be the Apostle to the Gentiles?
22. Q. What is the term most commonly applied to the Apostles in the New Testament Scriptures?
23. Q. What is the signification of the term "witness"?
24. Q. Where is the apostolic testimony recorded?

25. Q. What other special designation is given to the Apostles in the New Testament Scriptures?

26. Q. What is the signification of the term "ambassador"?

27. Q. How were the Apostles specially qualified for the work they were sent out to do?

28. Q. For what purpose were the gifts and powers of the Holy Spirit bestowed upon the Apostles in such great measure?

29. Q. Did the Apostles have any successors?

30. Q. What, firstly, did God do through the Apostles?

31. Q. What, secondly, did God do through the Apostles?

32. Q. What, thirdly, did God do through the Apostles?

33. Q. What, fourthly, did God do through the Apostles?

Lesson Forty-Two

THE ESTABLISHMENT OF THE CHURCH

Scripture Reading: Matt. 16:13-20; Acts 2:37-47.

Scriptures to Memorize: "Upon this rock I will build my church; and the gates of Hades shall not prevail against it" (Matt. 16:18). "They then that received his word were baptized: and there were added unto them in that day about three thousand souls" (Acts 2:41).

34. Q. What do we mean by the Christian Institution?

A. By the Christian Institution, we mean the Institution divinely established and appointed for the worship and service of God through Jesus Christ, throughout the Christian Dispensation.

Rom. 12:1—"I beseech you therefore, brethren, by the mercies of God, to present your bodies a living sacrifice, holy, acceptable to God, which is your spiritual service."

1 Cor. 6:19, 20—"Ye are not your own; for ye were bought with a price; glorify God therefore in your body." 1 Pet. 2:5—"ye also, as living stones, are built up a spiritual house, to be a holy priesthood, to offer up spiritual sacrifices, acceptable to God through Jesus Christ." Eph. 2:19-22, "So then ye are no more strangers and sojourners, but ye are fellow-citizens with the saints, and of the household of God, being built upon the foundation of the apostles and prophets, Christ Jesus himself being the chief corner stone; in whom each-several building, fitly framed together, groweth into a holy temple in the Lord; in whom ye also are builded together for a habitation of God in the Spirit." Heb. 10:25—"not forsaking our own assembling together, as the custom of some is, but exhorting one another; and so much the more, as ye see the day drawing nigh."

35. Q. What is the Christian Institution?

A. The Christian Institution is the Church of Christ.

Eph. 3:21—"Unto him be the glory in the church and in Christ Jesus unto all generations for ever and ever." Acts 20:28—"the church of the Lord which he purchased with his own blood." Heb. 11:23—"the general assembly and church of the firstborn who are enrolled in heaven."

36. Q. What is the derivation of the word "church"?

A. The word "church" in its derivative sense, means literally "whatever belongs or pertains to the Lord."

The word **church** (English), **kirk** (Scotch), **kirche** (German), is but a corruption of the Greek word **kuriakos**, and means, primarily, **belonging to the Lord**. This word was at first most likely used as an adjective for the purpose of defining the noun **ekklesia**, which among the ancients, denoted **an assembly** of any kind. It was only natural, therefore, that the Greek Fathers should have combined the two original words, in order to more clearly indicate the Church

of Christ as "the assembly of the Lord" or "the Lord's assembly."

37. Q. What, then, is the Church of Christ?

**A. The true Church of Christ is the body of obedi-
ent believers under the New Covenant who belong to God through Christ.**

(1) The true Church takes in all who are **in Christ**. Rom.
8:1—"there is therefore now no condemnation to them
that are in Christ Jesus." 2 Cor. 5:17—"if any man is in
Christ, he is a new creature." Gal. 3:26, 27—"For ye are
all sons of God through faith, in Christ Jesus. For as many
of you as were baptized into Christ, did put on Christ."
To be **in Christ**, is to be **in the Church of Christ**, and vice
versa; for the Church is the body of Christ. (2) It will
thus be seen that the **Kingdom** is a more comprehensive
term than the Church, in the fact that it takes in those
elect of God who cannot, in the very nature of the case,
belong to the Church; such as (a) the saved of all preceding dispensations; and (b) the innocent and irresponsible,
including infants, of all dispensations. Eph. 4:8—"when
he ascended on high, he led captivity captive." Mark 10:14
—"Suffer the little children to come unto me ... for to
such belongeth the kingdom of God."

**38. Q. Did the Church of Christ exist in Old Testament
times?**

**A. No. There was no such institution as the Church
of Christ in Old Testament times.**

The institution of worship in the Patriarchal Dispensation
was the Altar. In the Jewish Dispensation, it was the Tabernacle, the Temple, and the Synagogue, in succession.
These institutions were forerunners of the Church, and, in
certain respects, were typical of it. But the Church of
Christ itself was not established in either of the Old Testament Dispensations. To speak of the Hebrew Theocracy

as the "Jewish Church," as some do, is unscriptural and misleading.

39. Q. Was the Church of Christ established in the time of John the Baptizer?

    A. No. John's ministry was to the Jewish nation, and under the Mosaic law.

40. Q. Did Jesus Himself establish the Church while He was on earth?

    A. No. The personal ministry of Jesus Christ was under the Old Covenant and, likewise, under the Mosaic law.

The personal ministry of the Incarnate Word was under the Law of Moses, to which He rendered a faultless obedience. By His death on the Cross, He abrogated the Covenant of Law and ratified the Covenant of Grace. Col. 2:14 —"having blotted out the bond written in ordinances that was against us, which was contrary to us; and he hath taken it out of the way, nailing it to the cross."

41. Q. When was the Christian Institution set up?

    A. It was set up on the first Pentecost after the resurrection of Christ, A. D. 30.

(1) The word **church** is found only twice in the Gospel narratives of Matthew, Mark, Luke and John, viz., (a) in Matt. 18:17, where Jesus describes the procedure that is to be followed in effecting reconciliation between brethren; and (b) in Matt. 16:18, where Jesus says: "Upon this rock I will build my church." It will be noted that in this last-quoted text Jesus Himself refers to the Church as yet a thing of the future. He says: **will build,** not **have built;** thus precluding all such notions as, that the Church was established in the time of Adam, Abraham, or Moses, etc. This statement also disproves the theory that the Church was established in the time of John the Baptizer, for John had already been beheaded when these words were spoken. Moreover, the Scriptures teach clearly that the personal

ministry of Jesus was under the Law (Matt. 5:17-18); hence the Church, which is distinctly a New Testament institution, could not have been established until the Old Covenant had been abrogated and the New ratified and established by the death of Christ. (2) Beginning with the book of Acts, therefore, and throughout the rest of the New Testament Scriptures, the Church is alluded to repeatedly, and always as an established and functioning institution. As a matter of facts, Acts of Apostles is the history of the establishment, direction and expansion of the Church, under apostolic preaching and guidance. (3) It is quite generally admitted today that the Church of Christ was established on the day of Pentecost, A. D. 30, when the Holy Spirit descended in fulfilment of promise, when **the Gospel was proclaimed in fact** for the first time and sinners were first accepted into covenant relationship with God, through Christ, on the specific terms and conditions **of the New Testament. (See Acts, ch. 2.)** Acts 2:41— "they then that received his word were baptized; and there were added unto them (literally, **added together**) in that day about three thousand souls." Cf. Acts 2:47—"And the Lord added to them (literally, **added together**) day by day those that were saved" (literally, **those that were being saved**). This language clearly describes the incorporation of the body of Christ, the Church. From this time on, in the book of Acts and in the Epistles, the Church is invariably referred to as an established and functioning institution.

42. Q. **What positive proof have we that the Church of Christ was established on the day of Pentecost, A. D. 30?**

A. **The fact that the Holy Spirit descended on the day of Pentecost, A. D. 30, to incorporate the Church, to indwell it and vitalize it, and to enter upon His work of realizing and consummating**

God's Plan of Redemption for man, is the final and positive proof that the Church was established on that day.

(1) If the Church existed prior to the descent of the Holy Spirit on the day of Pentecost, as described in the second chapter of Acts, it was a lifeless institution; as dead, in fact, as the body of man was, which Jehovah God formed of the dust of the ground, before He breathed into it the breath of life (Gen. 2:7). For it was on this first Pentecost after the resurrection of our Lord, that the Spirit descended for the purpose of incorporating, vitalizing and indwelling the body of Christ. The language of Acts 2:41-47, as shown above, clearly describes the **forming of the body,** i. e., the incorporation of the Church. Where there is Spirit, there is life; hence the true Church is not an organization, but an **organism.** That is, it is a body of obedient believers in Christ, **vitalized** by the indwelling and abiding presence of the Spirit of God. (See John 7:37-39, Joel 2:28, Luke 24:45-49, Acts 1:1-8, Acts 2, etc.) From these facts it is obvious that there could not have been any church in existence, in the New Testament sense of the term, prior to the advent of the Holy Spirit, on Pentecost, A. D. 30. (2) The first thing the Holy Spirit did on that day was to bestow His gifts and powers in baptismal measure upon the Apostles, thus qualifying them for the work that Christ Himself had called them to do. The next thing the Spirit did, on that day, was to reveal the facts, commands and promises of the Gospel, through their preaching. The last thing He did was **to form into a body** the three thousand persons who heard the message on that day, who accepted its facts, repented of their sins, and submitted to Christian baptism. The Spirit's work on the day of Pentecost was threefold: (a) the qualifying of the Apostles for their task, (b) the revelation of the Gospel, with its facts, commands and promises; and (c) the incorporation of the Church of Christ. (3) Note the following summation of facts with

respect to the inauguration of the Christian Institution: "First, as a new covenant, it was ratified by the blood of Christ; as a testament, it was not a binding force while the testator lived; as a kingdom, it was not established until the King ascended and was crowned; as a church, its history shows that it was not organized while Jesus lived on earth; as the great salvation, it only 'began to be spoken by the Lord, and was confirmed unto us by them that heard him.' Finally, as the gospel, it was founded on the death, burial and resurrection of Christ, and was not preached until these facts had transpired" (Phillips, **The Church of Christ,** pp. 131-132).

43.   Q.   What, then, was the day of Pentecost, A.D. 30?

A.   It was the birthday of the Church of Christ.

(1) The point should be emphasized here that Christ Himself, through the instrumentality of His Apostles guided into all truth by the Holy Spirit, established His Church. In advance of its actual beginning, he said: "Upon this rock I will build my **church**" (Matt. 16:18). This Church had its inception on Pentecost, A. D. 30, at Jerusalem: and its history under the preaching and guidance of the Apostles is related in the book of Acts. (2) So, while the world thinks in terms of the Roman Church, of Luther's Church, of Calvin's Church, of Wesley's Church, etc., let us make it our special business to call attention to the fact that **our Lord Himself established a church;** that the church which He established is the true Church, the Church which He purchased with His own precious blood (Acts 20:28). (3) This Church was, and is, neither Greek Catholic, nor Roman Catholic, nor Protestant, nor a denomination of any kind whatsoever. It is Christ's Church, His body, the Church of Christ; the only Church authorized by the Scriptures. (4) Let us give ourselves unsparingly, therefore, to the great task of restoring and reproducing this Church in its original simplicity and purity, according to the pattern

laid down in the New Testament Scriptures. This is what we mean by "the restoration of primitive Christianity, its laws, ordinances and fruits."

44. Q. **What do we celebrate on the seventh Lord's Day after Easter each year?**

A. **We celebrate the anniversary of Pentecost, the birthday of the Church of Christ.**

It is our conviction that the anniversary of Pentecost, the birthday of the Church, should be observed annually with appropriate doctrinal messages, especially by those congre' gations which advocate the restoration of New Testament Christianity. Pentecost should be an outstanding day in the Christian calendar.

REVIEW EXAMINATION OVER LESSON FORTY-TWO

34. Q. **What do we mean by the Christian Institution?**
35. Q. **What is the Christian Institution?**
36. Q. **What is the derivation of the word "church"?**
37. Q. **What, then, is the Church of Christ?**
38. Q. **Did the Church of Christ exist in Old Testament times?**
39. Q. **Was the Church of Christ established in the time of John the Baptizer?**
40. Q. **Did Jesus Himself establish the Church while He was on earth?**
41. Q. **When was the Christian Institution set up?**
42. Q. **What positive proof have we that the Church of Christ was established on the day of Pentecost, A. D. 30?**
43. Q. **What, then, was the day of Pentecost, A.D. 30?**
44. Q. **What do we celebrate on the seventh Lord's Day after Easter each year?**

Lesson Forty-Three
THE CHURCH OF CHRIST

Scripture Reading: 1 Cor. 1:10-17, 3:1-11.

Scriptures to Memorize: "Neither for these only do I pray, but for them also that believe on me through their word; that they may all be one; even as thou, Father, art in me, and I in thee, that they also may be in us: that the world may believe that thou didst send me" (John 17:20-21). "There is one body, and one Spirit, even as also ye were called in one hope of your calling; one Lord, one faith, one baptism, one God and Father of all, who is over all, and through all, and in all" (Eph. 4:4-6).

---

45. Q. In what two general forms does the Church of Christ exist?

   A. It exists as: (1) the universal or catholic Church; and (2) the local church.

46. Q. What is the universal or catholic Church?

   A. The universal or catholic Church takes in all the elect of God under the New Covenant.

(1) The church universal is the body of Christ, the bride of Christ, the temple of God, the household of the faith, etc. As the word "catholic" means "universal," it follows that the only true catholic Church is the Church of Christ. (2) By "the elect of God" is meant: all obedient believers, or all who are truly in Christ. Rom. 8:1—"There is therefore now no condemnation to them that are in Christ Jesus," etc.

47. Q. What is the essential nature of the universal or catholic Church?

   A. It is essentially invisible, mystical, and spiritual.

(1) It is invisible in the sense that its "citizenship" is in heaven. Phil. 3:20—"For our citizenship is in heaven," etc.

Heb. 12:23—"the general assembly and church of the first-born who are enrolled in heaven." Rev. 13:8—"every one whose name hath not been written ... in the book of life of the Lamb that hath been slain." (2) It is **mystical** in the sense that its essential construction is beyond human understanding. John 10:14—here Jesus says: "I know mine own, and mine own know me." As Christ alone can discern the thoughts and intents of the human heart, He is the only one who can distinguish the truly believing and penitent, from those whose profession is merely nominal; hence He, in His capacity as Head of the church, must determine the constituency of His body. In the Scriptures, therefore, the Lord is said to do **the adding to** His own Church (Acts 2:47); and it follows that no one but He has the prerogative of **excommunication.** Eph. 2:21, 22—"in whom each several building, fitly framed together, groweth into a holy temple in the Lord; in whom ye also are builded together for a habitation of God in the Spirit." The actual construction of this "holy temple" is beyond human conception or description, and is known only to the Lord Himself; hence it can be described only by **metaphor,** such as the temple of God, the body of Christ, etc. (3) It is **spiritual,** in the sense that it is essentially holy. 1 Pet. 2:5—"Ye also, as living stones, are built up a spiritual house." Eph. 5:27—"a glorious church, not having spot or wrinkle or any such thing; but that it should be holy and without blemish."

48. Q. In what concrete form is the universal Church of Christ manifested in our visible world?

A. It concretes itself upon earth in the local church.

49. Q. What is the local church?

A. It is the assembly or congregation of obedient believers in a given community.

(1) Naturally the Church universal must have some sort of a local and visible manifestation, for practical purposes. This it has in the local congregation of Christians. (2)

The local church is the assembly or congregation of the saints in a given community, who are thus united and held together by the mutual bond of union with Christ and possession of the indwelling Spirit. 1 Cor. 12:27—"Now ye are the body of Christ, and severally members thereof." 1 John 1:7—"if we walk in the light, as he is in the light, we have fellowship one with another." Rom. 6:5—"if we have become united with him in the likeness of his death," etc. 2 Cor. 13:14—"the communion of the Holy Spirit, be with you all." (3) The local congregation exists and func-tions for purposes of fellowship, worship, service and evan-gelism. It is the concrete and practical manifestation of the Church catholic. Rom. 16:16—"the churches of Christ salute you." 1 Cor. 1:1—"unto the church of God which is at Corinth."

50.   Q.   What is the essential nature of the local church?

A.   It is essentially visible, temporal and practical.

(1) It is the local **recruiting-station**, where aliens are con-victed of sin and converted to righteousness through the preaching of the Gospel. (2) It is the spiritual **training-school**, in which the saints are nurtured in the admonition of the Lord (Eph. 6:4). (3) It is the local **assembly** of the saints for public worship. Heb. 10:25—"not forsaking our own assembling together." 1 Cor. 11:20—"when therefore ye assemble yourselves together." (4) It is the local **house-hold** of the faith, whose members come together on each first day of the week around the Family Table (the Lord's Table), to partake of the Family Feast of Remembrance (the Lord's Supper). See Acts 20:7, 1 Cor. 10:14-21, 11:20-33, etc. (5) It is not a museum for the exhibition of sanctimonious professors of religion, but a **workshop** for the shaping and forging of imperfect Christians into vessels meet for the inheritance of the saints (Col. 1:12). See 1 Pet. 2:2, 1 Cor. 3:2, 2 Pet. 3:18.

51.   Q.   In what visible form did the Church of Christ have its beginning?

A. The Church of Christ had its beginning in the local church at Jerusalem.

(1) This local church, established on the day of Pentecost, A. D. 30, was the **first** church of Christ in the world. Acts 8:1—"the church which was in Jerusalem." (2) As time went on, local churches sprang up and flourished in An-tioch, Iconium, Derbe, Lystra, Philippi, Thessalonica, Corinth, Ephesus, Rome, etc., in fact, in every community where the Gospel was preached. (3) Thus the Church universal, beginning from Jerusalem, increased and spread over the entire known world of apostolic times. The history of its rise and spread is related in the book of Acts of Apostles.

52. Q. **Was this first church, the church in Jerusalem, a Greek Catholic Church?**

     A. **No; for that was three centuries before the beginning of the Greek Catholic (Orthodox) Church.**

The history of the church in Jerusalem extended over the period from A. D. 30 to 70. The Greek Church did not come into existence until after the Council of Nicea, which was held in the year 325.

53. Q. **Was this first church, the church in Jerusalem, a Roman Catholic Church?**

     A. **No; for that was some six or seven centuries before the actual beginning of the Roman Church.**

Gibbon, **The History of the Decline and Fall of the Roman Empire,** Vol. II, traces the rise of the medieval Roman Hier-archy clearly (1) from the first Christian congregations in which the ministry of **bishop** (overseer) and that of **presby-ter** (elder) was one and the same (Acts 20:17-35); (2) to the gradual separation of the bishopric from the elder-ship, and the recognition of a ruling bishop in each local church; (3) to the recognition of the primacy of the metropolitan bishops; (4) to the establishment of the distinction between "clergy" and "laity";   (5) to the assertion of the claim of primacy over all other bishops by the Bishop of Rome. The union of church and state began to take shape with the Nicean Council, A. D. 325. The able and aggressive Leo (flourished about A. D. 450) was the most vigorous in pressing the claim of the primacy of the Roman bishopric. As early as A. D. 425, the Emperior Valentinian III had decreed that all the bishops of the West should obey the Bishop of Rome. In A. D. 533 the Emperor Justinian, by imperial edict, pro-claimed the Bishop of Rome the Head of the whole Church. The introduction of Latin worship capped this hierarchical development, about A. D. 666. However, the dogma of Papal Infallibility (ex cathedra) was not decreed until the Vatican Council of 1870.

54.   Q.   Was this first church, the church in Jerusalem, a Protestant Church?

A.   No; for that was some fourteen or fifteen centuries before the origin of Protestantism.

Protestantism had its beginnings in the work of such men as John Wyclif (1324-1384); John Huss (1369-1415); Sa-vonarola (1452-1498); Martin Luther (1483-1546); John Knox (1505-1572); John Calvin (1509-1564); Ulrich Zwingli (1484-1531); Philip Melanchthon (1497-1560), etc. The greatest of the later Reformers were John Wesley, George Fox, and Roger Williams.

55.   Q.   What, then, was this first church, the church in Jerusalem?

A.   It was a church of Christ.

(1) It was Christ's church, the church of Christ, in Jeru-salem. (2) Similarly, all local churches in apostolic times were called "churches of Christ." Rom. 16:16—"all the churches of Christ salute you."

56.   Q.   Was this first church, the church in Jerusalem, a

denomination? Or, was it affiliated with any denomination?

A.   No; it was undenominational, non-sectarian; for there were no denominations in apostolic times.

(1) It was just the church, Christ's church, Christ's body, in Jerusalem—nothing more, nothing less. (2) The word **denomination** means **division**, literally. There were no de-nominations in apostolic times, in the modern sense of the term. (3) The present-day denominational order is a hu-man addition to the true Church of Christ, and is the con-sequence of human apostasy, human theology, and human authority.

57.   Q.   What, then, is the Church revealed and described in the New Testament Scriptures?

A.   The Church described in the New Testament Scriptures is the Church of Christ.

It should be made so clear that your pupils will never forget it, that the Church of Christ was in existence long before there was such a thing as the Greek Catholic Church, or the Roman Catholic Church, or a Protestant Church, etc. It should be explained also, at this point, that the objective of the Restoration Movement is to reproduce the Church of Christ, in all its essential and permanent features, as revealed in the New Testament Scriptures.

58.   Q.   What, then, is the truth catholic Church?

A.   The true catholic or universal Church is the Church of Christ.

Hence the absurdity of a so-called "Roman Catholic" Church. How could the true catholic Church be "Roman" and "catholic" at the same time? If it is truly **catholic,** it cannot have any distinguishing or **denominational** aspects, such as "Greek," "Roman," "Anglican," Lutheran," "Epis-copalian," etc. The true catholic Church, the Church of Christ, is neither Roman, nor Greek, nor Anglican, nor

Protestant, nor denominational in any sense of the term. It is the body of Christ, which takes in all the elect of God under the New Covenant.

59. Q. Can we today belong to the Church of Christ without belonging to a denomination?

A. Certainly. We can belong to the Church of Christ by complying with the requirements, enjoined upon us by the Apostles themselves as necessary to salvation and union with Christ; and by continuing steadfastly in all the essentials of Christian worship and living as revealed in the New Testament Scriptures.

(1) The terms of admission into the Church of Christ are: belief in Christ, repentence from sin, confession of Christ, and baptism into Christ. See Mark 16:15-16; Matt. 28:18-20; Heb. 11:6; John 14:1; Acts 16:31; Acts 2:38; Luke 13:3; Acts 17:30; Acts 26:18; Matt. 10:32-33; Rom. 10:9-10; Acts 8:36-39; Acts 22:16; Rom. 6:3-5; Col. 2:12; Gal. 3:26-27; John 3:3-5, etc. (2) When we comply with the divine requirements laid down in the apostles' teaching as necessary to induct us **into Christ,** we are then **in the Church of Christ.** That is, the means by which we are inducted into Christ, also induct us into His body, the Church. For, according to New Testament teaching, all who are **in Christ** are **in His body** or Church, and **vice versa.** They are **Christians** therefore, nothing more, nothing else; and should continue steadfastly in all the essentials of Christian worship and living (Acts 2:42, Gal. 5:22-23). (3) To belong to a denomination, they must **add to** these scriptural requirements. They must affiliate with a human organization, submit to a man-made creed, adopt practices of human origin, and wear a human and **distinguishing** name. But this is not necessary. It is even more than unnecessary—it is **antiscriptural.** See Eph. 4:4-6; John 17:20-21; 1 Cor. 1:10, 3:1-3; etc.

60. Q. **What great lesson should we learn from these truths?**

A. **The lesson that we should be Christians only, and thus avoid contributing to the sin of denominationalism.**

(1) We should be Christians—not the **only** Christians, but **Christians** only. (2) We should take the New Testament Scriptures as our only guide in Christian faith, worship and practice. (3) We should "continue steadfastly in the apostles' teaching and fellowship, in the breaking of bread and the prayers" (Acts 2:42). (4) We should exemplify in our lives the fruit of the Holy Spirit (Gal. 5:22-23). (5) Thus "adorning the doctrine of God our Savior in all things" (Tit. 2:10), we should leave the first principles of Christ and press on unto perfection (Heb. 6:1). This is God's plan for us. May we live in harmony with it, and thus attain "the entrance into the eternal kingdom of our Lord and Savior Jesus Christ" (2 Pett. 1:11). (6) The notion one often hears expressed that denominationalism is "legitimate," "unavoidable," or even "God-designed," is absolutely without warrant in Scripture. On the contrary partyism is declared, by the Apostle Paul, to be evidence of carnality (1 Cor. 1:10-17, 3:1-8). "Factions, divisions, parties," etc., are listed in Scripture among "the works of the flesh": by no stretch of the imagination could these rightfully be categorized under the "fruit of the Spirit" (Gal. 5:19-24). Denominationalism is of human authority strictly: it has its roots in human speculative theology. It arose, of course, from the successive efforts of churchmen to find their way out of the morass of medieval hierarchism, dogmatism, and superstition, back to the purity of New Testament teaching and practice. In our day it is maintained almost entirely by the power of tradition. To love a denomination as such, that is, because of the tradition it embodies, is sectism pure and simple. Moreover, it is the

direct antithesis of our Lord's own prayer for the unity of His people (John 17:20-21).

REVIEW EXAMINATION OVER LESSON FORTY-THREE

45. Q. In what two general forms does the Church of Christ exist?

46. Q. What is the universal or catholic Church?

47. Q. What is the essential nature of the universal or catholic Church?

48. Q. In what concrete form is the universal Church of Christ manifested in our visible world?

49. Q. What is the local church?

50. Q. What is the essential nature of the local church?

51. Q. In what visible form did the Church of Christ have its beginning?

52. Q. Was this first church, the church in Jerusalem, a Greek Catholic Church?

53. Q. Was this first church, the church in Jerusalem, a Roman Catholic Church?

54. Q. Was this first church, the church in Jerusalem, a Protestant Church?

55. Q. What, then, was this first church, the church in Jerusalem?

56. Q. Was this first church, the church in Jerusalem, a denomination? Or, was it affiliated with any denomination?

57. Q. What, then, is the Church revealed and described in the New Testament Scriptures?

58. Q. What, then, is the truth catholic Church?

59. Q. Can we today belong to the Church of Christ without belonging to a denomination?

60. Q. What great lesson should we learn from these truths?

Lesson Forty-Four
THE CHURCH OF CHRIST (Concluded)

Scripture Reading: Eph. 2:10-22, 3:14-21, 5:22-33.

Scriptures to Memorize: "He put all things in subjection under his feet, and gave him to be head over all things to the church, which is his body, the fulness of him that filleth all in all" (Eph. 1:22-23). "Husbands, love your wives, even as Christ also loved the church, and gave himself up for it; that he might sanctify it, having cleansed it by the washing of water with the word, that he might present the church to himself a glorious church, not having spot or wrinkle or any such thing; but that it should be holy and without blemish" (Eph. 5:25-27). "Now unto him that is able to do exceeding abundantly above all that we ask or think, according to the power that worketh in us, unto him be the glory in the church and in Christ Jesus unto all generations for ever and ever. Amen" (Eph. 3:20-21).

---

61. Q. Who is the Head of the Church of Christ?

A. Christ Himself is the Head of the true Church.

Matt. 28:18—"All authority hath been given unto me in heaven and on earth." Eph. 1:22, 23—"and gave him to be head over all things to the church, which is his body." Eph. 5:23—"Christ also is the head of the church." See Eph. 4:15-16, Col. 1:18, Col. 2:10, etc. **The true Church of Christ has no other head.** Eph. 4:5—"**one Lord,** one faith, one baptism."

62. Q. Who is the Foundation of the Church of Christ?

A. Christ Himself is the Foundation of the true Church.

(1) Matt. 16:18—"upon this rock I will build my church," i. e., **upon the truth to which Peter had just given expression,** "Thou art the Christ, the Son of the living God."

This is the fundamental truth upon which the Church, the Gospel, in fact the entire Christian System, is built. To say that the Church rests upon the foundation of His Divine Sonship and Messiahship, is equivalent to saying that it is built **upon Christ Himself**. 1 Cor. 3:11—"For other foun' dation can no man lay than that which is laid, which is Jesus Christ." (2) Moreover, as the Apostles were ambas' sadors of Christ, the executors of His Last Will and Testa' ment, fully clothed with His authority and infallibility through the gifts and powers of the Holy Spirit bestowed upon them in baptismal measure; the Church is also said to have been erected upon the foundation of **the prophetic and apostolic testimony**, which is **the word of Christ**. Eph. 2:20—"being built upon the foundation of the apostles and prophets, Christ Jesus himself being the chief corner stone."

63.   Q.   What is the Creed of the Church of Christ?

A.   Christ Himself is the Creed of the true Church. John 20:31—"that ye may believe that Jesus is the Christ, the Son of God." Acts 16:31—"Believe on the Lord Jesus, and thou shalt be saved." John 14:1—"Ye believe in God, believe also in me." 2 Tim. 1:12—"for I know him whom I have believed." **The living Creed of the living Church of the living God is the ever-living Christ.** Rev. 1:17, 18—"I am the first and the last, and the Living One; and I was dead, and behold, I am alive for evermore, and I have the keys of death and of Hades."

64.   Q.   In what formula is this Creed expressed?

A.   In the formula: I believe that Jesus is the Christ, the Son of the living God.

(1) Matt. 16:16—"Thou art the Christ, the Son of the living God." This is the fundamental **truth** of Christianity, which in turn rests upon the fundamental fact of Christiani' ty, **that God raised up Jesus from the dead**. Rom. 10:9, 10 —"If thou shalt confess with thy mouth Jesus as Lord, and shalt believe in thy heart that God raised him from the dead,

thou shalt be saved: for with the heart man believeth unto righteousness; and with the mouth confession is made unto salvation." (2) The expression of this creedal formula by the individual, is the "good confession" (1 Tim. 6:13), which is made with the mouth (Rom. 10:9) unto salvation (Rom. 10:10). (3) Jesus is His name (Matt. 1:21). **Christ** is His title. The word **Christ** means **The Anointed One.** As prophets, priests and kings were anointed into office in olden times, it follows, that to confess Jesus as our Christ, is to accept Him as our Prophet, the Revealer of God, the One to whom we go for the words of eternal life (John 6:68); as our High Priest who maketh intercession for us at the right hand of God the Father (Heb. 7:25, 1 John 2:1, 1 Tim. 2:5); and as our King who has all authority over our lives (Matt. 28:18). (4) This Creed and its formula are both heaven-sent (John 1:14, 3:17; Matt. 16:17), scriptural, simple, comprehensive, and all-sufficient. **No other creeds or confessions are necessary.**

65. Q. What is the all-sufficient Discipline for the guidance of the true Church?

A. The all-sufficient Discipline for the guidance of the Church in faith and practice is the New Testament canon.

(1) The New Testament canon, i. e., the New Testament Scriptures as a whole, is the apostles' teaching, which is also the teaching of Christ as revealed by the Holy Spirit. John 16:13-15, 14:26, 20:21-23; Acts 2:4; 1 Cor. 2:1-15; 1 Cor. 14:37; 1 Thess. 2:13; 2 Tim. 3:16, etc. Acts 2:42— "and they continued stedfastly in the apostles' teaching," etc. (2) In the New Testament Scriptures "all things that pertain unto life and godliness" are fully revealed. 2 Pet. 1:3; cf. Jude 3. In 2 Tim. 3:16-17, we are told that the Scriptures are sufficient to furnish all Christians "completely unto every good work"; therefore no human additions are needed. The New Testament itself, which is **the word**

of Christ, is the authoritative and all-sufficient rule of faith and practice for the Church of Christ.

66. Q. What are the terms of admission into the Church of Christ?

A. They are: (1) belief in Christ, which includes the acceptance of Him as a personal Savior; (2) repentance from sin; (3) public confession of Christ; and (4) baptism into Christ.

(1) John 20:30-31, Acts 16:31, John 14:1. (2) Acts 2:38, Luke 13:3, Acts 17:30, Acts 26:18. (3) Matt. 10:32-33, Rom. 10:9-10, 1 Tim. 6:13. (4) Matt. 28:19, Mark 16:16; Acts 2:38, 8:36-39, 22:16; Rom. 6:3-5; Col. 2:12; Gal. 3:26-27; John 3:3-5, etc. (See Question 96.)

67. Q. What are the members of the Church of Christ called, in the New Testament Scriptures?

A. They are called disciples, believers, brethren, saints, priests, and Christians.

(1) Disciples, Acts 19:30. (2) Believers, Acts 5:14. (3) Brethren, 1 Cor. 6:8, 1 Tim. 4:6. (4) Saints, Rom. 1:7, 1 Cor. 1:2. (5) Priests, 1 Pet. 2:9; Rev. 5:10, 1:6, etc. (6) Christians, Acts 11:26, 26:28; 1 Pet. 4:16.

68. Q. What does the word "Christian" mean?

A. The word "Christian" means "of Christ" or "belonging to Christ."

69. Q. What names are given to the Church itself, in the New Testament Scriptures?

A. In its universal aspect, it is called "the church," "the church of God," "the church of the living God," "the church of the Lord," "the general assembly and church of the firstborn." Local congregations are called "churches," "churches of God," and "churches of Christ."

(1) Col. 1:18; 1 Cor. 15:9; 1 Tim. 3:5, 15; Acts 20:28; Heb. 12:23. (2) 1 Cor. 16:1; 1 Thess. 2:14; 1 Cor. 1:2; Rom. 16:16; Rev. 2:12, 18, etc.

70. Q. By what four great metaphors is the Church described, in the New Testament Scriptures?

A. It is spoken of as the temple of God, as the body of Christ, as the bride of Christ, and as the household of God.

(1) **The temple of God,** Eph. 2:21-22. This metaphor suggests dignity, solidarity, strength. (2) **The body of Christ,** 1 Cor. 12:27; Eph. 4:12, 1:22-23; Col. 1:24, etc. This metaphor suggests a fellowship of parts or members. (3) **The bride of Christ,** Eph. 5:22-33, Gal. 4:26; Rev. 21:2, 21:9, 22:17. This metaphor suggests purity, constancy, service, etc. (4) **The household of God;** or, **the household of the faith,** Eph. 2:19, Gal. 6:10. This metaphor suggests affinity of interest, purpose and work.

71. Q. What great lesson should we learn from these metaphors of the Church?

A. We should learn that the Church is most intimately related to Christ, and His partner in the great work of redeeming humanity; and that any one who ignores the Church or holds the Church in contempt cannot possibly please or honor Christ Himself.

Acts 20:28—"the church of the Lord, which he purchased with his own blood." Eph. 5:25—"Christ also loved the church, and gave himself up for it." And so we sing, in the words of Timothy Dwight:

> "I love Thy Church, O God;
>   Her walls before Thee stand,
> Dear as the apple of Thine eye,
>   And graven on Thy hand.
> For her my tears shall fall,
>   For her my prayers ascend,
> To her my cares and toils be given
>   Till toils and cares shall end."

REVIEW EXAMINATION OVER LESSON
FORTY-FOUR

61. Q. Who is the Head of the Church of Christ?

62. Q. Who is the Foundation of the Church of Christ?

63. Q. What is the Creed of the Church of Christ?

64. Q. In what formula is this Creed expressed?

65. Q. What is the all-sufficient Discipline for the guidance of the true Church?

66. Q. What are the terms of admission into the Church of Christ?

67. Q. What are the members of the Church of Christ called, in the New Testament Scriptures?

68. Q. What does the word "Christian" mean?

69. Q. What names are given to the Church itself, in the New Testament Scriptures?

70. Q. By what four great metaphors is the Church described, in the New Testament Scriptures?

71. Q. What great lesson should we learn from these metaphors of the Church?

Lesson Forty-Five
WHAT GOD IS DOING THROUGH THE CHURCH

Scripture Reading: Matt. 28:16-20, 24:3-14.

Scriptures to Memorize: "That thou mayest know how men ought to behave themselves in the house of God, which is the church of the living God, the pillar and ground of the truth" (1 Tim. 3:15). "And this gospel of the kingdom shall be preached in the whole world for a testimony unto all the nations; and then shall the end come" (Matt. 24:14).

72. Q. Who is the Administrator of the Church of Christ?

A. The Holy Spirit is the Administrator of the true Church.

(1) Christ is the Head of the Church. On His return to the Father, however, the Holy Spirit "came down from heaven" to act as His Agent. (2) The Holy Spirit came on the day of Pentecost to incorporate, indwell and administer the true Church throughout the present Dispensation. (3) The special work of the Holy Spirit in this Dispensation is to apply Christ's atoning work to the hearts of men, and to realize and consummate God's Plan of Redemption for man.

73. **Q. Through what means does the Holy Spirit administer the Church of Christ?**

A. He does so through the Word of Christ, i. e., the New Testament Scriptures.

(1) It is through the Word that the Holy Spirit (a) convicts sinners, and (b) sanctifies the saints. John 16:8— "And he, when he is come, will convict the world in respect of sin, and of righteousness, and of judgment." Cf. Acts 2:37. Col. 3:16—"Let the word of Christ dwell in you richly." (2) It is through the Word of Christ that the Holy Spirit organizes the local church, designates its officiary, and administers its affairs. Acts 20:28—"to all the flock, in which the Holy Spirit hath made you bishops," etc.

74. **Q. What are the three classes of officers authorized by the Holy Spirit for the local churches of Christ?**

A. They are: Evangelists, Elders, and Deacons.

(1) **Evangelists** are also spoken of as **ministers.** Acts 21:8, Eph. 4:11; 2 Tim. 4:5; 1 Tim. 4:6, etc. Evangelists are fundamentally preachers of the Gospel, bearers of the glad tidings, etc. 1 Tim. 5:17, 2 Tim. 4:12, 1 Cor. 1:21, Rom. 10:14, etc. (2) **Elders** are also known as **bishops, pastors, overseers, presbyters,** etc. Tit. 1:5-9; 1 Tim. 3:17; Acts

20:28; 1 Pet. 5:1-4; Phil. 1:1; Eph. 4:11; 1 Tim. 4:14, etc. To the elders of the local church is committed the spiritual leadership of the flock. (3) **Deacons**, Acts 6:1-6, Phil. 1:1, 1 Tim. 3:8-13. The word **deacon** means, literally, **servant.** Deacons are elected to look after the material and temporal interests of the local church. (4) It should be made clear at this point, that the **apostolic** and **prophetic** offices were extraordinary and temporary; that is, they belonged only to the infancy of the Church. The Apostles were witnesses and ambassadors of Christ, as we have already learned. (See Lesson Forty-One.) The prophets were inspired teachers. Acts 11:27, 13:1-2; Eph. 4:11. The apostolic and prophetic offices came to an end when the written Word was compiled and installed in the Church. We have the inspired Book, the New Testament Scriptures, which is truly **the apostles' teaching,** as our all-sufficient guide in religious faith and practice. 1 Cor. 13:8, Rom. 10:8, 2 Pet. 1:3, Jude 3, etc.

75. Q. What, firstly, is God doing through the Church?

   A. Through the Church of Christ, God is perpetuating and perfecting the essential laws, principles and institutions of true religion.

(1) Our Altar is Christ, the sacrificial Altar for all mankind. (2) Our Sacrifice is the Lamb of God Himself. John 1:29, 1 Cor. 5:7, Heb. 7:26-27, etc. (3) Our High Priest is Christ, and our Priesthood is a priesthood of all Christians. Heb. 9:11-12; 1 Pet. 2:5, 9; Rev. 1:6, 5:10; Heb. 13:15; Rom. 12:1.

76. Q. What, secondly, is God doing through the Church?

   A. Through the Church of Christ, God is preserving and perpetuating the means and appointments of true Christian worship.

77. Q. What are the means and appointments of true Christian worship?

A. **They are: (1) the preaching and teaching of the New Testament Scriptures, the apostles' teaching; (2) the contribution of tithes and offerings; (3) the Lord's Supper, or breaking of bread; and (4) prayer.**

(1) Acts 2:42—"they continued stedfastly in the apostles' teaching and fellowship, in the breaking of bread and the prayers." (2) **The apostles' teaching,** which is the word of Christ, was at first **oral,** but is now embodied in the New Testament Scriptures. It is to be taught and proclaimed by faithful men, 2 Tim. 2:2. (3) **Fellowship,** from the Greek word **koinonia,** which is rendered "contribution" in Rom. 15:26; and, in 2 Cor. 8:4, is given "the fellowship in the ministering to the saints." The term evidently alludes to the contribution and distribution of tithes and offerings, for the support of the ministry, the care of the needy, the aged, the distressed, etc. The offering is an essential part of Christian worship. 1 Cor. 16:1-2. (4) **The breaking of bread,** otherwise known as the Lord's Supper (1 Cor. 11:20), and as the Communion of the Body and of the Blood of Christ (1 Cor. 10:16). The Lord's Supper is a memorial of the Atonement; it commemorates and pictorializes the death and suffering of Christ (1 Cor. 11:23-26). It is the very heart and center of all true Christian worship. (5) **Prayer,** which is a necessary and vital part of true worship, and the only means which the Christian has to secure daily forgiveness of sin. Acts 8:22, 1 John 1:9, 1 John 2:1. 1 Thess. 5:17—"pray without ceasing."

78. Q. **What does Jesus say with regard to true worship?**

A. **He says: "God is a Spirit; and they that worship him must worship in spirit and truth" (John 4:24).**

That is, true worship is the communion of the human spirit with the Divine Spirit, according to the terms, means and appointments laid down in the Word of truth. For Christians, the Word of truth is the New Testament Scriptures.

79.   Q.   **Through what local institution does God thus perpetuate the means and appointments of true Christian worship?**

A.   **Through the local assembly or congregation of obedient believers, i. e., the local church.**

The church universal concretes itself on earth in the local congregation of Christians. It is through the local church that the means and appointments of true Christian worship are thus preserved; and not through a lodge, club, fraternity, or human society of any kind. 1 Cor. 11:20—"when therefore ye assemble yourselves together." Heb. 10:25—"not forsaking our own assembling together, as the custom of some is." Eph. 2:22—"ye also are builded together for a habitation of God in the Spirit."

80.   Q.   **What is the day divinely appointed for Christian worship and service?**

A.   **The first day of the week, known as the Lord's Day.**

Acts 20:7—"Upon the first day of the week, when we were gathered together to break bread," etc. Rev. 1:10—"I was in the Spirit on the Lord's day." The Lord's Day is essentially a memorial of the resurrection of Christ. Mark 16:9—"Now when he was risen early on the first day of the week," etc.

81.   Q.   **What, thirdly, is God doing through the Church?**

A.   **Through the Church of Christ, God is preserving and perpetuating His divine ordinances.**

82.   Q.   **What are the Christian ordinances?**

A.   **They are: Baptism, and the Lord's Supper.**

(1) **Baptism**, scripturally, is the immersion of a penitent believer in water, in obedience to the command of Christ. See Mark 16:16, Matt. 28:19-20, Acts 2:38, Acts 8:36-39, Col. 2:12, Rom. 6:3-4, etc. (2) The **Lord's Supper** is a me-

morial of the suffering and death of Christ on the Cross. See 1 Cor. 10:16, 11:23-26.

83. Q. Should we speak of Baptism and the Lord's Supper as "ordinances of the Church"?

A. No. They are ordinances of Christ, which He has ordained for the Church to keep.

Baptism and the Lord's Supper are not "ordinances of the Church." They were instituted by Christ Himself for the Church to observe in their original manner and frequency of observance. See Matt. 26:26-29, Luke 22:14-23, Matt. 28:19-20, Mark 16:16. No group of churchmen, clergymen, theologians or priests; no assembly, conference, council, synod or congregation has any right to change, in any particular whatsoever, the observance of the Lord's ordinances as described in the New Testament Scriptures. **They should be regarded as sacred trusts**, to be perpetuated by the Church in their original simplicity and purity.

84. Q. What, fourthly, is God doing through the Church?

A. Through the Church of Christ, God is preserving and perpetuating His Word of truth.

2 Tim. 2:19—"Howbeit the firm foundation of God standeth." Matt. 24:35—"Heaven and earth shall pass away, but my words shall not pass away." 1 Tim. 3:15—"the church of the living God, the pillar and ground of the truth." Departure from God's truth is **heresy**, and it is the duty of the Church to resist and expose heresy. 2 John 9:11, "Whosoever goeth onward and abideth not in the teaching of Christ, hath not God. . . . If any one cometh unto you, and bringeth not this teaching, receive him not into your house, and give him no greeting: for he that giveth him greeting partaketh in his evil works."

85. Q. What, fifthly, is God doing through the Church?

A. Through the Church of Christ, God is causing

the Gospel to be preached for a testimony unto all the nations.

Mark 16:15—"Go ye into all the world, and preach the gospel to the whole creation." Matt. 28:19—"Go ye there-fore, and make disciples of all the nations," etc. Matt. 24:14—"this gospel of the kingdom shall be preached in the whole world for a testimony unto all the nations; and then shall the end come." The field is the world.

86.   Q.   What, sixthly, is God doing through the Church?

A.   Through the Church of Christ, God is perpetu-ating and realizing His Plan of Redemption for mankind.

The Father originates and plans. The Son executes. The Spirit applies, realizes and consummates. So the Holy Spirit is the Agent of the Godhead throughout the present Dis-pensation, in applying the benefits of Christ's redemptive work to the hearts and lives of men and women; thus re-generating them, sanctifying them, and making them par-takers of the divine nature (2 Pet. 1:4), and fitting them for their eternal inheritance which is incorruptible and un-defiled, and which fadeth not away (1 Pet. 1:4). 1 Pet. 1:2 —"according to the foreknowledge of God the Father, in sanctification of the Spirit, unto obedience and sprinkling of the blood of Jesus Christ."

87.   Q.   What, then, is the twofold mission of the Church?

A.   The twofold mission of the Church of Christ is: (1) to preserve the truth of God in its simplicity and purity; and (2) to proclaim the truth of God for a testimony unto all the nations.

88.   Q.   What fundamental truth with regard to the Church should be impressed upon the minds of people of our day and age?

A.   The truth that the one and only institution in

which God has promised to enter into covenant relationship with men, throughout the Christian Dispensation, is the Church of Christ.

In saying this, we make no exceptions or qualifications. No man can hope to be saved on the ground of his morality, respectability, good citizenship, etc.; or in consequence of his social, fraternal, or political connections. We cannot be saved because we are good Masons, good Odd Fellows, good citizens, etc. Salvation is only in Christ; and to be in Christ, scripturally, is to be in the Church of Christ, which is his body. "Unto him be the glory in the church and in Christ Jesus unto all generations for ever and ever. Amen" (Eph. 3:21).

REVIEW EXAMINATION OVER LESSON FORTY-FIVE

72. Q. Who is the Administrator of the Church of Christ?

73. Q. Through what means does the Holy Spirit administer the Church of Christ?

74. Q. What are the three classes of officers authorized by the Holy Spirit for the local churches of Christ?

75. Q. What, firstly, is God doing through the Church?

76. Q. What, secondly, is God doing through the Church?

77. Q. What are the means and appointments of true Christian worship?

78. Q. What does Jesus say with regard to true worship?

79. Q. Through what local institution does God thus perpetuate the means and appointments of true Christian worship?

80. Q. What is the day divinely appointed for Christian worship and service?

81. Q. What, thirdly, is God doing through the Church?

82. Q. What are the Christian ordinances?

83. Q. Should we speak of Baptism and the Lord's Supper as "ordinances of the Church"?

84. Q. What, fourthly, is God doing through the Church?

85. Q. What, fifthly, is God doing through the Church?

86. Q. What, sixthly, is God doing through the Church?

87. Q. What, then, is the twofold mission of the Church?

88. Q. What fundamental truth with regard to the Church should be impressed upon the minds of people of our day and age?

Lesson Forty-Six
THE GOSPEL OF CHRIST

Scripture Reading: Acts 2:22-36, 1 Cor. 15:1-11.

Scriptures to Memorize: "For I am not ashamed of the gospel: for it is the power of God unto salvation to everyone that believeth" (Rom. 1:16). "But though we, or an angel from heaven, should preach unto you any gospel other than that which we preached unto you, let him be anathema" (Gal. 1:8).

89. Q. What message is the Church commissioned to preach to all nations?

    A. The Gospel (Matt. 28:19-20, Mark 16:15-16).

90. Q. What does the word "gospel" mean?

    A. The word "gospel" means "good news" or "glad tidings."

91. Q. What is the Gospel of Christ?

    A. It is the good news about Christ and about salvation in His name.

Luke 2:10, 11—"Behold, I bring you good tidings of great joy which shall be to all the people: for there is born to you this day in the city of David a Savior, who is Christ the Lord." Acts 4:12—"in none other is there salvation: for neither is there any other name under heaven, that is given among men, wherein we must be saved." Acts 10:43—"to him bear all the prophets witness, that through his name every one that believeth on him shall receive remission of sins." Acts 8:12—"But when they believed Philip preaching good tidings concerning the kingdom of God and the name of Jesus Christ, they were baptized, both men and women."

92. Q. **What does the Gospel of Christ include?**

A. **It includes (1) three facts to be believed, (2) three commands to be obeyed, and (3) three gifts to be enjoyed.**

(1) Mark 1:14—"believe in the gospel." 1 Cor. 15:1-4, "Now I make known unto you, brethren, the gospel which I preached unto you. . . . For I delivered unto you first of all that which also I received: that Christ died for our sins according to the scriptures; and that he was buried; and that he hath been raised on the third day according to the scriptures," etc. (2) Rom. 10:16—"they did not all hearken to the glad tidings" (A. V.—"they have not all obeyed the gospel"). 2 Thess. 1:8—"rendering vengence to them that know not God, and to them that obey not the gospel of our Lord Jesus." That which is to be obeyed must of necessity **have commands.** (3) Jas. 1:17—"every good and every perfect gift is from above." Rom. 11:29—"for the gifts and the calling of God are not repented of." Eph. 4:8—"When he ascended on high, he led captivity captive, and gave gifts unto men."

93. Q. **What are the three great facts of the Gospel?**

A. **The three great facts of the Gospel are the death, burial and resurrection of Christ.**

1 Cor. 15:3, 4—"that Christ died for our sins according to the scriptures; and that he was buried; and that he hath

been raised on the third day according to the scriptures."
Acts 2:23, 24, 32—"him, being delivered up by the de'
terminate counsel and foreknowledge of God, ye by the
hand of lawless men did crucify and slay: whom God raised
up, having loosed the pangs of death. . . . This Jesus did
God raise up, whereof we all are witnesses." Rom. 5:8—
"while we were yet sinners, Christ died for us." Acts
10:39, 40—"whom also they slew, hanging him on a tree.
Him God raised up the third day," etc.

**94. Q. Who were the divinely appointed witnesses of
these three facts of the Gospel?**

A. The Apostles.

Acts 1:22, 1:8, 2:32, 10:40'41, etc. (See Questions 22'24
inclusive.)

**95. Q. When were the facts of the Gospel first pro-
claimed as such?**

A. On the day of Pentecost, A. D. 30.

(1) From Adam to Abraham, the Gospel existed in the
purpose of God only. It was at first merely intimated (in
the mysterious oracle of Gen. 3:15). Eph. 6:19—"the mys'
tery of the gospel." Eph. 3:4, 5—"the mystery of Christ,
which in other generations was not made known," etc. Eph.
3:11—"the eternal purpose which he purposed in Christ
Jesus." (2) From Abraham to Isaiah, the Gospel existed
in **promise.** It was preached to Abraham, we are told; but
only in promise. Gal. 3:8. (3) From Isaiah to Malachi,
the Gospel existed in **prophecy,** i. e., in the Messianic pre'
dictions of the Hebrew prophets. See Isa. 9:6'7, 53:1'9,
etc. Cf. 1 Pet. 1:10'12. (4) During the personal ministry
of Jesus, the Gospel was in process of **preparation**; hence
it was called "the gospel of the kingdom" (Matt. 4:23),
i. e., the good news that the kingdom of heaven was **at hand**
(Matt. 3:2, 10:7). (5) It is obvious, however, that the
facts of the Gospel could not have been proclaimed **as facts**
prior to their actual occurrence; that is, not until after

Jesus died and was raised up from the dead. Hence we find that the Gospel was actually proclaimed for the first time, **in fact**, on the first Pentecost after the resurrection of our Lord. See Acts 2:22-36.

96. Q. What are the three great commands of the Gospel?

A. They are: believe on the Lord Jesus, repent, and be baptized.

(1) Acts 16:31—"Believe on the Lord Jesus, and thou shalt be saved." Mark 16:16—"He that believeth and is baptized shall be saved." John 20:30-31, 14:1, etc. (2) Luke 13:3 —"Except ye repent, ye shall all in like manner perish." Acts 3:19—"Repent ye therefore, and turn again, that your sins may be blotted out." Acts 17:30—"The times of ig-norance therefore God overlooked; but now he command-eth men that they should all everywhere repent." Acts 26:18—"to open their eyes, that they may turn from dark-ness to light and from the power of Satan unto God, that they may receive remission of sins," etc. (3) Acts 2:38— "Repent ye, and be baptized every one of you in the name of Jesus Christ unto the remission of your sins." Cf. Mark 16:16, Matt. 28:19, Gal. 3:26-27, Rom. 6:3-4, etc.

97. Q. What are the three great gifts of God offered to man through the Gospel?

A. They are: remission of sins, the indwelling of the Holy Spirit, and eternal life.

(1) Acts 2:38—"Repent ye, and be baptized every one of you in the name of Jesus Christ unto the remission of your sins." Acts 10:43—"through his name every one that be-lieveth on him shall receive remission of sins." Luke 24:47 —"that repentance and remission of sins should be preached in his name unto all the nations, beginning from Jerusalem." Eph. 2:8—"for by grace have ye been saved through faith; and that not of yourselves, it is the gift of God" (i. e., it is **salvation** that is the gift of God; cf. John 3:16). (2) John

7:39—"this spake he of the Spirit, which they that believed on him were to receive." Acts 2:38—"Repent ye, and be baptized . . . unto the remission of your sins, and ye shall receive the gift of the Holy Spirit" (i. e., the Holy Spirit as a gift). Rom. 5:5—"the love of God hath been shed abroad in our hearts through the Holy Spirit which was given unto us." 1 Cor. 3:16—"Know ye that . . . the Spirit of God dwelleth in you?" 1 Cor. 6:19—"Know ye not that your body is a temple of the Holy Spirit, which is in you, which ye have from God?" 2 Cor. 1:22—"God, who also sealed us, and gave us the earnest of the Spirit in our hearts." (3) Rom. 5:21—"that, as sin reigned in death, even so might grace reign through righteousness unto eternal life through Jesus Christ our Lord." Matt. 25:46—"these shall go away into eternal punishment; but the righteous into eternal life" (Jesus). Rom. 6:23—"the free gift of God is eternal life in Christ Jesus our Lord."

98.   Q.   What is the fundamental truth of the Gospel?

A.   The fundamental truth of the Gospel is that Jesus is the Christ, the Son of the living God.

This truth was first confessed by Simon Peter (Matt. 16:16 —"Thou art the Christ, the Son of the living God"). This is the truth which must be confessed by all who would be saved from their sins. John 20:30, 31—"Many other signs therefore did Jesus in the presence of the disciples, which are not written in this book; but these are written, that ye may believe that Jesus is the Christ, the Son of God; and that believing ye may have life in his name." Matt. 10:32, 33—"Every one therefore who shall confess me before men, him will I also confess before my Father who is in heaven. But whosoever shall deny me before men, him will I also deny before my Father who is in heaven."

99.   Q.   What is the most fundamental fact of the Gospel?

A.   The most fundamental fact of the Gospel is that

God raised His Son Jesus Christ from the dead.

(1) Matt. 16:18—"I also say unto thee that thou art Peter, and upon this rock I will build my church: and the gates of Hades shall not prevail against it." The rock upon which the Church is built, is the **truth**, first voiced by Peter (Matt. 16:16), that Jesus is the Christ, the Son of the living God. Had Jesus gone into the grave and not come forth, the gates of Hades (the grave) would have prevailed against the truth that He is the Christ, the Son of the living God. But the fact hat He did come forth from the grave, that God raised Him up, that death had no dominion over Him, is the final and positive proof that He was all that He claimed to be—the Christ, the Son of the living God. Rom. 1:4—"who was declared to be the Son of God with power . . . by the resurrection from the dead; even Jesus Christ our Lord." Acts 2:24—"whom God raised up, having loosed the pangs of death: because it was not possible that he should be holden of it." Cf. Acts 2:32-36. (2) Thus the fundamental truth of the Gospel rests upon the fundamental fact of the Gospel. Rom. 10:9-10—"If thou shalt confess with thy mouth Jesus as Lord, and shalt believe in thy heart that God raised him from the dead, thou shalt be saved: for with the heart man believeth unto righteousness, and with the mouth confession is made unto salvation."

100. Q. **What is the fundamental requirement of the Gospel?**

A. **The fundamental requirement of the Gospel is obedience to Christ.**

Matt. 17:5—"This is my beloved Son, in whom I am well pleased; hear ye him." John 15:14—"Ye are my friends, if ye do the things which I command you." John 14:15—"If ye love me, ye will keep my commandments." Heb. 5:9—"he became unto all them that obey him the author of eternal salvation." Cf. Mattt. 7:24-27.

101. Q. What is the most fundamental gift or reward of the Gospel?

  A. The most fundamental gift or reward of the Gospel is eternal life.

2 Tim. 1:9, 10—"our Savior Christ Jesus, who abolished death, and brought life and immortality to light through the gospel." John 17:3—"This is life eternal, that they should know thee the only true God, and him whom thou didst send, even Jesus Christ." John 3:36—"He that be' lieveth on the Son hath eternal life; but he that obeyeth not the Son shall not see life, but the wrath of God abideth on him." 1 John 5:12—"He that hath the Son hath the life; he that hath not the Son of God hath not the life." Cf. John 3:16, 2 Pet. 1:11.

102. Q. By what various designations is the Gospel described in the New Testament Scriptures?

  A. By various designations which indicate its divine origin, content and design.

It is called "the gospel" (Rom. 1:16); "the gospel of Jesus Christ, the Son of God" (Mark 1:1); "the gospel of the grace of God" (Acts 20:24); "the gospel of God" (Rom. 1:1); "the gospel of his Son" (Rom. 1:9); "the gospel of Christ" (1 Cor. 9:12, Gal. 1:7); "the gospel of the glory of Christ" (2 Cor. 4:4); "the word of the truth, the gospel of your salation" (Eph. 1:13); and "eternal good tidings" (Rev. 14:6).

103. Q. What does God do through the Gospel?

  A. Through the Gospel He calls men to remission of sins and eternal life in Christ Jesus our Lord.

2 Thess. 2:13-14, "But we are bound to give thanks to God always for you, brethren beloved of the Lord, for that God chose you from the beginning unto salvation in sancti' fication of the Spirit and belief of the truth: whereunto he called you through our gospel, to the obtaining of the glory of our Lord Jesus Christ."

104. Q. What does Paul say about the Gospel?

A. He says that the Gospel is the power of God unto salvation to every one that believeth (Rom. 1:16).

(1) Note that is not a power, nor **one** of the powers, but **the** power of God unto salvation. (2) Cf. 1 Cor. 1:21—"it was God's good pleasure through the foolishness of the preaching to save them that believe."

105. Q. Why is the Gospel the power of God unto salvation?

A. It is the power of God unto salvation because the Holy Spirit is in it and operates through it.

(1) The Holy Spirit exerts His influences and powers through the Gospel, to convict sinners and to sanctify Christians. The principle of spiritual life embodied in the Gospel is the presence and power of the Spirit therein; hence, we are exhorted to receive witth meekness the implanted word which is able to save our souls (Jas. 1:21). (2) The presence and power of the Holy Spirit in the Bible sets it apart from all other books; distinguishes Scripture from all other literature. The presence of the Holy Spirit in the Church sets it apart from all human institutions. The presence of the Holy Spirit in the Gospel distinguishes it from all human messages and systems. Let us therefore thank God for the glad tidings.

"Publish glad tidings, tidings of peace,
Tidings of Jesus, redemption and release."

106. Q. How may we enjoy the wonderful gifts of God that are offered to us through the Gospel?

A. We may enjoy them by believing the facts of the Gospel, by obeying the commands of the Gospel, and by continuing steadfastly in all the exercises and appointments of Christian faith, worship and practice.

2 Pet. 1:10, 11—"Wherefore, brethren, give the more dili-
gence to make your calling and election sure: for if ye do
these things, ye shall never stumble; for thus shall be richly
supplied unto you the entrance into the eternal kingdom of
our Lord and Savior Jesus Christ." Rev. 2:7—"To him
that overcometh, to him will I give to eat of the tree of life,
which is in the Paradise of God." Rev. 2:11—"He that
overcometh shall not be hurt of the second death." Let us
therefore cherish the Gospel of Christ, and devote ourselves
zealously to its proclamation; for we are told that "they
that are wise shall shine as the brightness of the firmament;
and they that turn many to righteousness as the stars for
ever and ever" (Dan. 12:3).

> "Should all the forms which men devise
>   Attack my faith with treacherous art,
>   I'd call them vanity and lies,
>   And bind the gospel to my heart."

REVIEW EXAMINATION OVER LESSON
FORTY-SIX

89. Q. What message is the Church commissioned to
preach to all nations?

90. Q. What does the word "gospel" mean?

91. Q. What is the Gospel of Christ?

92. Q. What does the Gospel of Christ include?

93. Q. What are the three great facts of the Gospel?

94. Q. Who were the divinely-appointed witnesses of
these three facts of the Gospel?

95. Q. When were the facts of the Gospel first proclaimed as such?

96. Q. What are the three great commands of the
Gospel?

97. Q. What are the three great gifts of God offered
to man through the Gospel?

98. Q. What is the fundamental truth of the Gospel?

99. Q. What is the most fundamental fact of the Gospel?

100. Q. What is the fundamental requirement of the Gospel?

101. Q. What is the most fundamental gift or reward of the Gospel?

102. Q. By what various designations is the Gospel described in the New Testament Scriptures?

103. Q. What does God do through the Gospel?

104. Q. What does Paul say about the Gospel?

105. Q. Why is the Gospel the power of God unto salvation?

106. Q. How may we enjoy the wonderful gifts of God that are offered to us through the Gospel?

Lesson Forty-Seven

THE PROPHETIC OFFICE OF CHRIST

Scripture Reading: John 4:15-26, 14:1-10; Acts 3:19-26.

Scriptures to Memorize: "No man hath seen God at any time; the only begotten Son, who is in the bosom of the Father, he hath declared him" (John 1:18). "I and the Father are one" (John 10:30). "He that hath seen me hath seen the Father" (John 14:9). "God . . . hath at the end of these days spoken unto us in his Son" (Heb. 1:1-2).

---

107. Q. What was the name given to the Son of God to indicate the nature and design of His work in the world?

A. The name Jesus.

"Jesus" means "Savior." This name was given by Divine authorization. Matt. 1:21—"Thou shalt call his name Jesus; for it is he that shall save his people from their sins" (the words of the Annunciating Angel, to Joseph).

108. Q. What is His official title?

A. **His official title is: Christ.**

109. Q. **What does this title mean?**

A. **"Christ" means "The Anointed One."**

The terms "Messiah" (Hebrew), "Christos" (Greek), and "Christ" (English), all mean "The Anointed One." A great many people have the idea that "Christ" is a part of His name, and hence use the words "Jesus Christ" in the same manner as, for instance, "George Washington." This is erroneous. To illustrate: "Edward King" may be the name of a man; but "Edward the King" would indicate a monarch. So, "Jesus" was the name divinely bestowed upon the Son of God, but "Christ" is His official title. Jesus the Christ (or Jesus Christ) is, then, The Anointed One of God, the King of kings and Lord of lords (1 Tim. 6:14-15).

110. Q. **What three classes of rulers were inducted into office, in Old Testament times, by the ceremony of anointing?**

A. **The prophets, priests, and kings.**

111. Q. **What was the design of the ceremony of anointing?**

A. **It was the outward sign of investiture to sacred office.**

(1) It was the custom by Divine warrant in Old Testament times, to solemnly anoint into office all those who were called to be prophets, priests, and kings. See Exo. 28:41; Lev. 16:32; 1 Sam. 9:16, 15:1, 16:12-13; 1 Kings 19:15-16, etc. (2) This anointing was emblematic of investiture to sacred office, and of particular sanctification or designation to the service of God. To anoint meant, says Cruden, "to consecrate and set one apart to an office" (**Concordance**). (3) The element used in the ceremony of anointing was olive oil (Exo. 30:22-25). This "holy anointing oil" was typical of the comforting and strengthening gifts and powers of the Holy Spirit.

112. Q. When did the Anointing of Jesus take place?

A. It took place immediately after His baptism.

113. Q. How was His divine anointing signified to the world?

A. It was signified by the descent of the Holy Spirit upon Him.

(1) Necessarily His Anointing took place at the beginning of His ministry. Matt. 3:16, 17—"And Jesus, when he was baptized, went up straightway from the water: and lo, the heavens were opened unto him, and he saw the Spirit of God descending as a dove, and coming upon him; and lo, a voice out of the heavens, saying, This is my beloved Son, in whom I am well pleased." (2) The Anointing of Jesus was a matter of Old Testament prediction. See Psa. 45:7; Heb. 1:9; Isa. 61:1; Luke 4:16-19. (3) Acts 4:27— "Against the Lord, and against his Anointed." Acts 10:38 —"even Jesus of Nazareth, how God anointed him with the Holy Spirit and with power," etc. (4) The ceremony of anointing, in olden times, often preceded that of corona- tion by a considerable period of time, as, for instance, in David's case. Hence, while the Anointing of Jesus took place at the beginning of His ministry, His Coronation did not occur until after His resurrection from the dead.

114. Q. What, then, is the special signification of His title, "Christ"?

A. This title describes Him in His threefold offi- cial capacity, as Prophet, Priest, and King of His Church.

() "One particularly designed and chosen by God, to be the King, Priest and Prophet of His church, namely, Christ Jesus; who was filled with the Holy Ghost in an extraordi- nary manner, and thereby consecrated and authorized to be the Messiah" (Cruden, **Concordance**). (2) Make it clear at this point, that to confess Jesus as "the Christ, the Son of the living God," is to accept Him as Prophet to whom we go for the words of eternal life; as Priest, who offered Himself as the Perfect Sacrifice for sin, and who continually makes intercession for us; and as King who has all authority over our hearts and lives. Note the profound import and comprehensiveness of "the good confession."

115. Q. What is a prophet, in the scriptural sense of the term?

A. A prophet, in scripture, is one who reveals the will of God to man.

"Here we must avoid the narrow interpretation which would make a prophet a mere foreteller of future events. He was rather an inspired interpreter of the divine will, a medium of communication between God and men" (Strong, **Systematic Theology**, p. 710). E. g., Abraham (Gen. 20:7); the patriarchs (Psa. 105:15); John the Baptizer (Matt. 11:9-10); New Testament interpreters and expounders of the Scriptures (1 Cor. 12:28; Eph. 2:20, 3:5, 4:11, etc.).

116. Q. What are the four essential functions of the prophetic office?

A. They are: (1) revelation; (2) instruction, or teaching; (3) prediction; and (4) demonstration, or miracle-working.

The true prophet was one who revealed the will of God to his people; one who instructed his people in the essentials of righteousness and holy living; one who foretold important future events; and one who authenticated his ministry by performing miracles.

117. Q. In what sense was Jesus pre-eminently the Prophet of God?

A. In the sense that He exercised the functions of the prophetic office perfectly.

(1) He was the final and perfect revelation of God to mankind. John 1:18—"No man hath seen God at any time; the only begotten Son . . . he hath declared him." John

8:26—"howbeit he that sent me is true; and the things which I heard from him, these speak I unto the world." John 14:9—"he that hath seen me hath seen the Father." Cf. John 17:8, Heb. 1:1-2, etc. (2) He is the Supreme Teacher of all time. Mark 1:22—"they were astonished at his teaching: for he taught them as having authority, and not as the scribes." John 7:46—"Never man so spake." No one has ever been able to add anything to the body of moral and spiritual truth which He left in the world. (3) He foretold significant future events, such as (a) the circumstances of His own betrayal, suffering, death, and resurrection (Matt. 9:15, 17:12, 17:22-23, 20:17-19, 26:1-2, 26:10-12, 26:33-34; Mark 8:31, 9:9; Matt. 26:20-25; Luke 9:44, 11:29-32, 13:31-35; Mark 9:31; John 3:14-15, 2:19-22, 6:70-71, 16:32, etc.); (b) His ascension to heaven (John 6:62, 7:33-34, 16:5-7); (c) His ultimate return in power and glory (Matt. 26:63-64, John 14:3); (d) the advent of the Holy Spirit (John 7:37-39, 14:16-18, 14:26, 15:26, 16:7-10; Luke 24:49); (e) the growth and progress of His kingdom (Matt. 13:31-33; Mark 4:26-29, 9:1); (f) the destruction of Jerusalem (Luke 19:41-44, 23:28-31); (g) the complete destruction of the Temple (Matt. 24:1-2); (h) the rejection of the Jews and their dispersion among all peoples (Matt. 21:42-45, 23:35-39; Luke 21:20-24); (i) the calling of the Gentiles (Matt. 8:11-12, John 10:16); (j) the precursors of His second coming and of the end of our age (Matt. 13:24-30, 13:36-43, 13:47-50, 11:21-23, 24:3-14, 24:15-22, 24:29-31, 24:32-44; Luke 21:10-11, 21:25-28, etc.) Many of these predictions have already been literally fulfilled. (4) God also authenticated His ministry and work by many wonderful miracles. Acts 2:22 —"Jesus of Nazareth, a man approved of God unto you by mighty works and wonders and signs which God did by him in the midst of you." Note the wide variety of His miracles **as to kind**: the stilling of the tempest, the feeding of a multitude with a few loaves and fishes, the turning of water into wine, the blasting of the fig tree, the casting out of demons, the healing of the sick, the raising of the dead, etc. He had but to command, and all Nature obeyed His voice.

118.   Q.   In what Old Testament scripture is the prophetic office and work of Christ foretold?

A.   It is foretold by Moses, in Deut. 18:15-19.

Cf. John 4:16-19, Matt. 21:11, Acts 3:22-26, etc.

119.   Q.   What was the first stage of Christ's prophetic work?

A.   It was His preparatory work, as the Word of God, in enlightening mankind, prior to His advent in the flesh.

John 8:58—"Before Abraham was born, I am." Col. 1:16, 17—"for in him were all things created . . . and he is before all things, and in him all things consist." In 1 Cor. 10:4, it is said that the children of Israel under Moses "drank of a spiritual rock that followed them: and the rock was Christ." For instances of preincarnate manifestations of the Word of God (the Logos), see Gen. 14:17-20, Heb. 7:1-3; Gen. 18:1-22; Josh. 5:13-15; Judg. 13:6-7; Dan. 3:24-25, etc. We must not forget that all preparatory and preliminary knowledge of God given to man in the early ages of the world, came from the Word Himself, who has always been the Revealer of God.

120.   Q.   What was the second stage of Christ's prophetic work?

A.   It was His ministry and work in the flesh.

In His earthly ministry, Christ was the Prophet **par excellence.** "While He submitted, like the Old Testament prophets, to the direction of the Holy Spirit, unlike them, He found the sources of all knowledge and power within Himself. The word of God did not **come** to Him: He was **Himself** the Word" (Strong, **Systematic Theology,** p. 712). See

John 1:18, 8:26, 14:9, 17:8; Heb. 1:1-2, etc. His entire ministry in the flesh was a revelation of the wisdom, power, holiness, love and compassion of the heavenly Father.

121. Q. What is the third stage of Christ's prophetic work?

A. It is His continued direction and guidance of His Church on earth, since His ascension to the Father.

His prophetic activity is thus continued: (a) through the agency of the Holy Spirit, (b) by means of His word as revealed in the New Testament Scriptures, and (c) through the instrumentality of His prophets, apostles and ministers. See John 16:13-15; Acts 1:1-3, 2:1-4; Rom. 10:6-10; Eph. 4:11-16; 2 Tim. 2:2, 4:1-5, etc. John 6:63—"the words that I have spoken unto you are spirit, and are life." Matt. 24:35—"Heaven and earth shall pass away, but my words shall not pass away."

122. Q. What will be the final stage of Christ's prophetic work?

A. It will be His final revelation of the Father to His saints in glory.

John 16:25—"The hour cometh, when I shall no more speak unto you in dark sayings, but shall tell you plainly of the Father." 1 Cor. 13:12—"Now we see in a mirror, darkly; but then face to face: now I know in part; but then shall I know fully even as also I was fully known." Rev. 21:23—"And the city hath no need of the sun, neither of the moon, to shine upon it; for the glory of God did lighten it, and the lamp thereof is the Lamb." "Thus Christ's prophetic work will be an endless one, as the Father whom He reveals is infinite" (Strong, **ibid.**, p. 712.).

REVIEW EXAMINATION OVER LESSON FORTY-SEVEN

107. Q. What was the name given to the Son of God

to indicate the nature and design of His work in the world?

108. Q. What is His official title?

109. Q. What does this title mean?

110. Q. What three classes of rulers were inducted into office, in Old Testament times, by the ceremony of anointing?

111. Q. What was the design of the ceremony of anointing?

112. Q. When did the Anointing of Jesus take place?

113. Q. How was His divine anointing signified to the world?

114. Q. What, then, is the special signification of His title, "Christ"?

115. Q. What is a prophet, in the scriptural sense of the term?

116. Q. What are the four essential functions of the prophetic office?

117. Q. In what sense was Jesus pre-eminently the Prophet of God?

118. Q. In what Old Testament scripture is the prophetic office and work of Christ foretold?

119. Q. What was the first stage of Christ's prophetic work?

120. Q. What was the second stage of Christ's prophetic work?

121. Q. What is the third stage of Christ's prophetic work?

122. Q. What will be the final stage of Christ's prophetic work?

Lesson Forty-Eight
THE PRIESTLY OFFICE OF CHRIST

Scripture Reading: Heb. 7:20-28, 9:23-28.

Scriptures to Memorize: "Wherefore it behooved him in all things to be made like unto his brethren, that he might become a merciful and faithful high priest in things pertaining to God, to make propitiation for the sins of the people" (Heb. 2:17). "For such a high priest became us, holy, guileless, undefiled, separated from sinners, and made higher than the heavens" (Heb. 7:26). "Wherefore also he is able to save to the uttermost them that draw near unto God through him, seeing he ever liveth to make intercession for them" (Heb. 7:25).

---

123. Q. In what Old Testament scripture is the priestly office and work of Christ foretold?

A. It is foretold in Psalm 110:4.

Psa. 110:4—"Jehovah hath sworn, and will not repent: Thou art a priest for ever, after the order of Melchizedek." Cf. Gen. 14:18-20; Heb. 5:6, 5:10, 6:20, 7:1-3, etc.

124. Q. What book of the New Testament treats especially of the Priesthood of Christ?

A. The Epistle to the Hebrews.

125. Q. What was one reason why the Word became flesh and dwelt among us?

A. It was that He might, in His capacity of Prophet, reveal God to mankind.

John 1:18 8:26, 14:9, 17:8; Heb. 1:1-2.

126. Q. What was a second reason why the Word became flesh and dwelt among us?

A. It was that He might, in His capacity of King, destroy the works of the devil, deliver His peo-

ple from the bondage of sin and death, and
bring many sons unto glory.

1 John 3:8—"To this end was the Son of God manifested,
that he might destroy the works of the devil." Heb. 2:9,
10—"But we behold him who hath been made a little low-
er than the angels, even Jesus, because of the suffering of
death crowned with glory and honor, that by the grace of
God he should taste death for every man. For it became
him, for whom are all things, in bringing many sons unto
glory, to make the author of their salvation perfect through
sufferings." 1 Cor. 15:25, 26—"For he must reign, till he
hath put all enemies under his feet. The last enemy that
shall be abolished is death."

**127. Q. What was a third reason why the Word be-
came flesh and dwelt among us?**

    **A. It was that He might acquaint Himself with
our frailties, and thus qualify Himself to act as
our merciful and faithful High Priest.**

Heb. 2:14-18, "Since then the children are sharers in flesh
and blood, he also himself in like manner partook of the
same; that through death he might bring to nought him
that had the power of death, that is, the devil; and might
deliver all them who through fear of death were all their
lifetime subject to bondage ... Wherefore it behooved him
in all things to be made like unto his brethren, that he
might become a merciful and faithful high priest in things
pertaining to God, to make propitiation for the sins of the
people. For in that he himself hath suffered being tempted,
he is able to succor them that are tempted."

**128. Q. What is a priest, in the scriptural sense of the
term?**

    **A. A priest, according to scripture, is a person di-
vinely appointed to transact with God on be-
half of man.**

129. Q. What are the three essential qualities which a priest must possess?

A. They are: power or authority, purity, and sympathy.

130. Q. To what extent do these qualities inhere in Christ?

A. They inhere in Christ pre-eminently and perfectly.

(1) His **power** or **authority.** Matt. 9:6—"But that ye may know that the Son of man hath authority on earth to forgive sins," etc. Matt. 28:18—"All authority hath been given unto me in heaven and on earth. Heb. 7:24—"he, because he abideth for ever, hath his priesthood unchangeable." His authority is "not after the law of a carnal commandment, but after the power of an endless life" (Heb. 7:16); that is, it is inherent in His Divine nature as the eternal Word, the only begotten Son of God, etc. Cf. John 8:58, 1:1-3; Rev. 1:17-18. (2) His **purity.** Heb. 7:26—"For such a high priest became us, holy, guileless, undefiled, separated from sinners, and made higher than the heavens." Heb. 7:28—"For the law appointeth men high priests, having infirmity; but the word of the oath, which was after the law, appointeth a Son, perfected for evermore." (3) His **sympathy.** Heb. 4:15—"For we have not a high priest that cannot be touched with the feeling of our infirmities; but one that hath been in all points tempted like as we are, yet without sin." Heb. 2:17, 18—"Wherefore it behooved him in all things to be made like unto his brethren, that he might become a merciful and faithful high priest in things pertaining to God, to make propitiation for the sins of the people. For in that he himself hath suffered being tempted, he is able to succor them that are tempted."

131. Q. What are the two essential functions of a priest, according to the Scriptures?

A. They are (1) to offer sacrifice, and (2) to make intercession.

132. Q. What sacrifice for sin did Christ offer up, acting in His capacity of High Priest?

A. He offered up Himself as the Supreme Sacrifice and as the Perfect Atonement for the sins of the world.

(1) Heb. 7:27—"who needeth not daily, like those high priests, to offer up sacrifices, first for his own sins, and then for the sins of the people: for this he did once for all, when he offered up himself." Heb. 9:24-26, "For Christ entered not into a holy place made with hands, like in pattern to the true; but into heaven itself, now to appear before the face of God for us: nor yet that he should offer himself often, as the high priest entereth into the holy place year by year with blood not his own; else must he often have suffered since the foundation of the world; but now once at the end of the ages hath he been manifested to put away sin by the sacrifice of himself." Heb. 10:12 —"but he, when he had offered one sacrifice for sins for ever, sat down on the right hand of God." (2) While this Supreme Sin-offering was made for all mankind, its benefits and blessings are only for those who accept Him as their Savior and obey his commands. (Point out, in this connection, that any sort of a gift must be accepted before it can be enjoyed). Heb. 5:9—"having been made perfect, he became unto all them that obey him the author of eternal salvation."

133. Q. Why was His Sacrifice a Perfect Sin-offering?

A. It was a Perfect Sin-offering, because He Himself, the Lamb of God, was "holy, guileless and undefiled" (Heb. 7:26).

Heb. 9:14—"How much more shall the blood of Christ, who through the eternal Spirit offered himself up without

blemish unto God, cleanse your conscience from dead works
to serve the living God?"

**134. Q. What other work does Christ do for His peo-
ple, in His capacity as their High Priest?**

**A. He makes intercession for them at the right
hand of God.**

"The Priesthood of Christ does not cease with His work
of atonement, but continues forever. In the presence of God
He fulfils the second office of the priest, namely that of
intercession" (Strong, **Systematic Theology**, p. 773). Heb.
7:23-25, "And they indeed have been made priests many
in number, because that by death they are hindered from
continuing: but he, because he abideth for ever, hath his
priesthood unchangeable. Wherefore also he is able to
save to the uttermost them that draw near unto God
through him, seeing he ever liveth to make intercession for
them." 1 John 2:1—"If any man sin, we have an Advocate with the Father, Jesus Christ the righteous." Rom.
8:34—"It is Christ Jesus that died, yea rather, that was
raised from the dead, who is at the right hand of God, who
also maketh intercession for us." In view of this continuous intercession of our unchangeable High Priest, we
should, as Christians, "have boldness to enter into the holy
place by the blood of Jesus, by the way which he dedicated
for us, a new and living way, through the veil, that is to
say, his flesh; and having a great priest over the house of
God; let us draw near with a true heart in fulness of faith,
having our hearts sprinkled from an evil conscience: and
having our body washed with pure water" (Heb. 10:19-
22).

**135. Q. Since Christ exercises the function of High
Priest, who, then, are His subordinate priests
under the New Covenant?**

**A. The Scriptures teach that all Christians are
priests.**

(1) 1 Pet. 2:5—"ye also, as living stones, are built up a spiritual house, to be a holy priesthood, to offer up spiritual sacrifices, acceptable to God through Jesus Christ." 1 Pet. 2:9—"ye are an elect race, a royal priesthood." Rev. 1:5, 6 —"unto him that loveth us, and loosed us from our sins by his blood; and he made us to be a kingdom, to be priests unto his God and Father." (2) There is neither command nor precedent for a special order of priests under the Coven-ant of Grace. Matt. 23:9—"Call no man your father on the earth; for one is your Father, even he who is in heaven."

136. Q. What is our privilege as priests unto God?

   A. It is our privilege and joy to offer up to God our spiritual sacrifices of prayer, praise, thanks-giving, devotion, and service.

1 Pet. 2:5—"to offer up spiritual sacrifices." Rom. 12:1— "I beseech you therefore, brethren, by the mercies of God, to present your bodies a living sacrifice, holy, acceptable to God, which is your spiritual service." Heb. 13:15— "through him then let us offer up a sacrifice of praise con-tinually, that is, the fruit of lips which make confession to his name."

REVIEW EXAMINATION OVER LESSON FORTY-EIGHT

123. Q. In what Old Testament scripture is the priestly office and work of Christ foretold?

124. Q. What book of the New Testament treats es-specially of the Priesthood of Christ?

125. Q. What was one reason why the Word became flesh and dwelt among us?

126. Q. What was a second reason why the Word be-came flesh and dwelt among us?

127. Q. What was a third reason why the Word be-came flesh and dwelt among us?

128. Q. What is a priest, in the scriptural sense of the term?

129. Q. What are the three essential qualities which a priest must possess?

130. Q. To what extent do these qualities inhere in Christ?

131. Q. What are the two essential functions of a priest, according to the Scriptures?

132. Q. What sacrifice for sin did Christ offer up, acting in His capacity of High Priest?

133. Q. Why was His Sacrifice a Perfect Sin-offering?

134. Q. What other work does Christ do for His people, in His capacity as their High Priest?

135. Q. Since Christ exercises the function of High Priest, who, then, are His subordinate priests under the New Covenant?

136. Q. What is our privilege as priests unto God?

Lesson Forty-Nine
THE KINGLY OFFICE OF CHRIST

Scripture Reading: Isa. 9:6-7; Eph. 2:15-23; 1 Cor. 15:20-28.

Scriptures to Memorize: "Wherefore also God highly exalted him, and gave unto him the name which is above every name; that in the name of Jesus every knee should bow, of things in heaven and things on earth and things under the earth, and that every tongue should confess that Jesus Christ is Lord, to the glory of God the Father" (Phil. 2:9-11). "Our Lord Jesus Christ ... who is the blessed and only Potentate, the King of kings, and Lord of lords" (1 Tim. 6:14-15). "For he must reign, till he hath put all his enemies under his feet. The last enemy that shall be abolished is death" (1 Cor. 15:25-26).

137. Q. What, according to scripture, is the order of Christ's priesthood?

A. The Scriptures teach that Christ's Priesthood is after the order of Melchizedek.

(1) Psa. 110:4—"Jehovah hath sworn, and will not re-pent: Thou art a priest for ever after the order of Mel-chizedek." Cf. Heb. 5:10, 6:20, 7:17, etc. Heb. 7:1-3, "For this Melchizedek, king of Salem, priest of God Most High, who met Abraham returning from the slaughter of the kings and blessed him, to whom also Abraham divided a tenth part of all (being first, by interpretation, King of righteousness, and then also King of Salem, which is, King of peace; without father, without mother, without geneal-ogy, having neither beginning of days nor end of life, but made like unto the Son of God), abideth a priest continual-ly." (2) For the story of Abraham and Melchizedek, see Gen. 14:18-20.

138. Q. In what sense is the Priesthood of Christ after the order of Melchizedek?

A. In the twofold sense that it is (1) an eternal Priesthood, and (2) a royal Priesthood.

(1) Heb. 7:15, 16—"after the likeness of Melchizedek there ariseth another priest, who hath been made, not after the law of a carnal commandment" (as the Levitical priest-hood was), "but after the power of an endless life." Heb. 6:20—"having become a high priest for ever after the order of Melchizedek." The Priesthood of Christ is eternal, be-cause Christ Himself is eternal. (2) Again, Melchizedek. was both "King of Salem" and "Priest of God Most High." So Christ, the antitype of Melchizedek, is **both King and Priest** of His people. He exercises the functions of both offices; His Priesthood is, therefore, a royal Priesthood.

139. Q. In what Old Testament scriptures is the kingly office and work of Christ foretold?

A. In numerous Old Testament scriptures, as, for example, Psa. 110:1, 2:6, 45:6; Isa. 9:6-7, etc.

140. Q. What do we mean by the Kingship of Christ?

A. **By the Kingship of Christ, we mean His Sovereignty as the Divine-Human Redeemer.**

Not His sovereignty as the eternal Word, but His sovereignty as The Anointed One of God.

141. Q. **Did Christ exercise His sovereignty while He was in the flesh?**

A. **He manifested it quite frequently, both in the natural and in the spiritual realms.**

(1) He had but to speak and the natural world obeyed Him. E. g., the stilling of the tempest, the multiplying of a few loaves and fishes into sufficient food for a multitude, the cursing of the fig tree, the healing of the bodies of men, etc. Matt. 8:27—"What manner of man is this, that even the winds and the sea obey him?" (2) He also, while in the flesh, frequently exercised His right to forgive sins. Matt. 9:6—"But that ye may know that the Son of man hath authority on earth to forgive sins," etc. To the penitent thief on the cross, He said: "Today shalt thou be with me in Paradise" (Luke 23:43). Cf. Matt. 9:2, Luke 7:48, etc.

142. Q. **By what special miracle did God prove the sovereignty of Christ to the world?**

A. **He proved it by raising Him up from the dead.**

Rom. 1:3, 4—"Concerning his Son ... who was declared to be the Son of God with power, according to the spirit of holiness, by the resurrection from the dead; even Jesus Christ."

143. Q. **When did Christ begin to exercise fully the powers and prerogatives of His kingly office?**

A. **He did so when He entered upon His state of exaltation.**

(1) While He was in the flesh—i. e., in His state of humiliation—He was, so to speak, "the uncrowned King." It was not until after His resurrection and ascension that

He was vested with the scepter of the Kingdom and crowned King of kings and Lord of lords. (2) Eph. 1:19' 22, "according to that working of the strength of his might which he wrought in Christ, when he raised him from the dead, and made him to sit at his right hand in the heavenly places, far above all rule, and authority, and power, and dominion, and every name that is named, not only in this world, but also in that which is to come: and he put all things in subjection under his feet, and gave him to be head over all things to the church," etc. Acts 2:32, 33—"This Jesus did God raise up ... being therefore by the right hand of God exalted," etc. Rom. 14:9—"For to this end Christ died and lived again, that he might be Lord of both the dead and the living."

144. Q. Why is it impossible for sinners to be saved today in the same manner that the penitent thief on the cross was saved?

A. For the simple reason that, since the death of Christ, sinners are to receive pardon according to the provisions and terms of His Last Will and Testament.

Christ was here in person when He spoke pardon to the penitent thief. While He was in the flesh, He had the authority, and frequently exercised it, to forgive sins as He saw fit. While a man still lives, he has the right to dis' pense his possessions as he chooses; but after his death his property must be distributed according to the provisions of his will or testament. So, while Jesus was on earth in per' son, acting as the representative of the Godhead in execut' ing the scheme of redemption, as God in the flesh He had the authority to forgive sins by a spoken word. But when He became obedient unto death and then returned to the Father in glory, He made provisions for the blessings and benefits of Divine grace to be dispensed according to the terms of His Last Will and Testament. See Mark 16:16, Acts 2:38, Rom. 10:9-10, etc.

145. Q. What is the essential nature of Christ's Kingdom?

A. It is essentially spiritual in its nature.

(1) It is not geographical, political, economic, etc. Nor is it essentially **social.** John 18:36—"My kingdom is not of this world." Rom. 14:17—"The kingdom of God is not eating and drinking, but righteousness and peace and joy in the Holy Spirit." (2) It is essentially **spiritual.** It is the kingdom of the truth (John 18:37); and its location is in the human heart. Luke 17:20, 21—"the kingdom of God cometh not with observation . . . the kingdom of God is within you."

146. Q. What is Christ's Kingdom, in its temporal aspect?

A. In its temporal aspect it is the Kingdom of Grace.

147. Q. What is Christ's Kingdom, in its eternal aspect?

A. In its eternal aspect, it is the Kingdom of Glory.

2 Pet. 1:11—"the entrance into the eternal kingdom of our Lord and Savior Jesus Christ." 2 Tim. 4:18—"the Lord will . . . save me unto his heavenly kingdom."

148. Q. What are the essential characteristics of Christ's rule?

A. Christ's rule is (1) spiritual, and (2) absolute.

(1) His Kingship is **spiritual,** in the sense that it is in the human heart. (2) His Kingship is **absolute,** in the sense that His will is the law from which there is no appeal. His Kingdom is an **absolute monarchy.** Matt. 28:18—"All authority hath been given unto me in heaven and on earth." "All" here means, not part, but **all.**

149. Q. In what respect is the Kingdom broader in scope than the Church?

A. In the respect that it takes in the innocent and
irresponsible who, in the very nature of the
case cannot belong to the Church.

E. g., infants, who cannot belong to the Church because
of their inability to believe and obey, can and do belong
to the Kingdom, by virtue of the fact that when Christ died
on the Cross, He atoned for the innocent and irresponsible,
unconditionally. Luke 18:16—"Suffer the little children
to come unto me, and forbid them not: for to such belongeth the kingdom of God."

150. Q. What office does Christ hold in relation to the
Church, in consequence of His Kingship.

A. He is the Head of the Church, which is His
body.

Eph. 1:22-23, 4:15; Eph. 5:23; Col. 1:18, etc.

151. Q. Does the Church have any other Head than
Christ?

A. The true Church has only one Head—Christ
Himself.

Christ the Head, and the Church the Body, together make
up the total Mystic Personality, in and through whom human redemption is effected. The Body with two Heads
would be as great a monstrosity as the Head with some
two hundred bodies (denominations?). The Church has
no need of any other Head than Christ Himself. Obviously, therefore, the self-styled "Visible Head of the Church"
who occupies "St. Peter's Chair" is a creation of human
authority pure and simple. The Papacy is a man-originated
institution without any Scripture warrant whatever. (Cf.
2 Thess. 2:1-4, 1 Tim. 4:1-5, etc.). Eph. 4:4-6, "There is
one body, and one Spirit, even as also ye were called in one
hope of your calling; one Lord, one faith, one baptism, one
God and Father of all," etc.

152. Q. How long shall Christ continue in His capacity
of Acting Sovereign?

A. The Scriptures teach that He shall reign until every enemy of God and man, including death itself, shall have been conquered.

1 Cor. 15:25, 26—"For he must reign, till he hath put all his enemies under his feet. The last enemy that shall be abolished is death."

153. Q. What will Christ ultimately do with His Sovereignty?

A. The Scriptures teach that He will ultimately transfer His Sovereignty back to the Father, that God may be all in all.

1 Cor. 15:24, 28—"Then cometh the end, when he shall deliver up the kingdom to God, even the Father; when he shall have abolished all rule and all authority and power . . . And when all things have been subjected under him, then shall the Son also himself be subjected to him that did subject all things unto him, that God may be all in all."

REVIEW EXAMINATION OVER LESSON FORTY-NINE

137. Q. What, according to scripture, is the order of Christ's priesthood?

138. Q. In what sense is the Priesthood of Christ after the order of Melchizedek?

139. Q. In what Old Testament scriptures is the kingly office and work of Christ foretold?

140. Q. What do we mean by the Kingship of Christ?

141. Q. Did Christ exercise His sovereignty while He was in the flesh?

142. Q. By what special miracle did God prove the sovereignty of Christ to the world?

143. Q. When did Christ begin to exercise fully the powers and prerogatives of His kingly office?

144. Q. Why is it impossible for sinners to be saved today in the same manner that the penitent thief on the cross was saved?

145. Q. What is the essential nature of Christ's King-
          dom?
146. Q. What is Christ's Kingdom, in its temporal
          aspect?
147. Q. What is Christ's Kingdom, in its eternal aspect?
148. Q. What are the essential characteristics of Christ's
          rule?
149. Q. In what respect is the Kingdom broader in scope
          than the Church?
150. Q. What office does Christ hold in relation to the
          Church, in consequence of His Kingship.
151. Q. Does the Church have any other Head than
          Christ?
152. Q. How long shall Christ continue in His capacity
          of Acting Sovereign?
153. Q. What will Christ ultimately do with His Sov-
          ereignty?

Lesson Fifty
THE END OF OUR AGE

Scripture Reading: Acts 1:1-10; Matt. 24:3-14;
Heb. 9:23-28.

Scriptures to Memorize: "This Jesus, who was received
up from you into heaven, shall so come in like manner as
ye beheld him going into heaven" (Acts 1:11). "So Christ
also, having been once offered to bear the sins of many,
shall appear a second time, apart from sin, to them that
wait for him, unto salvation" (Heb. 9:28). "He who
testifieth these things saith, Yea: I come quickly. Amen:
come, Lord Jesus" (Rev. 22:20).

154. Q. What do we mean by "the end of our age"?
      A. By "the end of our age," we mean the end of
          the present or Christian Dispensation.

155. Q. When will the Christian Dispensation end?

A. The Christian Dispensation will end when Christ comes again.

Matt. 24:14, Matt. 24:37-39, Acts 1:11, Heb. 9:28, etc.

156. Q. Is the doctrine of the Second Coming of Christ prominent in the Scriptures?

A. It is one of the most outstanding doctrines of the New Testament Scriptures.

(1) The Second Coming is said to be "the blessed hope" of every true Christian (Tit. 2:11-14). (2) Those who study what the Scriptures teach with reference to this subject are said to be "blessed" (Rev. 1:3). (3) One verse in every twenty-five in the New Testament, mentions or alludes to the Second Coming. (4) Jesus Himself had much to say about His return. See Matt. 25:1-13, 14-30; Matt. 24:3-51; Mark 13:3-8, 14-37; Luke 17:22-37, 21:10-36, 12:35-48, etc. (5) The closing words of the New Testament anticipate the Lord's return. Rev. 22:20—"Come, Lord Jesus."

157. Q. What do the Scriptures teach with respect to the nature of the Second Coming?

A. The Scriptures teach that the Second Coming of Christ will be (1) personal, (2) outward and visible, and (3) glorious.

(1) Personal, i. e., not merely in political, social, reformatory or religious movements. The Lord will come Himself. 1 Thess. 4:16—"For the Lord Himself shall descend from heaven"; cf. Acts 1:11. (2) Outward and visible. Rev. 1:7—"he cometh with the clouds; and every eye shall see him." John 5:28—"all that are in the tombs shall hear his voice." "We do not know how all men at one time can see a bodily Christ; but we also do not know the nature of Christ's body ... The telephone has made it possible for men widely separated to hear the same voice; it is equally

possible that all men may see the same Christ coming in the clouds" (Strong, **Systematic Theology**, p. 1005). May we not reasonably conclude that such inventions as the radio and television are but preparatory for this glorious event? (3) **Glorious.** Luke 21:27—"Then shall they see the Son of man coming in a cloud with power and great glory." He will come in Majesty: not as the suffering Savior, but as the reigning Sovereign. See 2 Thess. 1:7, Mark 8:38, Luke 9:26, Tit. 2:13, etc.

158. Q. What do the Scriptures teach with regard to the time of the Second Coming?

A. The Scriptures teach that the exact time of Christ's Second Coming is not revealed to man.

(1) Matt. 24:36—"But of that day and hour knoweth no man, not even the angels of heaven, neither the Son, but the Father only." Acts 1:7—"It is not for you to know times or seasons, which the Father hath set within his own authority." (2) The exact time of the Second Coming has been purposely concealed from us, for three reasons: (a) to prevent irreligiousness followed by last-minute reformation; (b) to stimulate in the hearts of His people the blessed hope of His appearing; and (c) to heighten their anticipation of the glorious event. See Mark 13:33-37: "Take ye heed, watch and pray ... and what I say unto you, I say unto all, Watch!"

159. Q. What are to be the purposes of the Second Coming?

A. The Scriptures teach that Christ will come to complete His conquest of evil in all its forms, and to complete the salvation of His people.

(1) He comes to expose sin in all its forms (1 Cor. 4:5).
(2) He comes to judge the nations (Isa. 2:4, Acts 17:31).
(3) He comes to destroy the Anti-christ (2 Thess. 2:8).
(4) He comes to receive His Bride, the True Church, unto Himself (1 Thess. 4:16-17, Eph. 5:25-27, Rev. 19:7-8).

(5) He comes to glorify His saints (1 Cor. 15:22-23). (6)
He comes to reign until Satan shall have been subjugated
and his evil works abolished (1 Cor. 15:25-26, Rev. 20:1-
3). (7) He comes to gloriously consummate God's eternal
purpose and plan (Acts 3:20-21). Cf. 1 John 3:8, Rev.
22:12, etc.

160. **Q. What conditions are to prevail throughout the
world immediately prior to the Second Coming
of Christ?**

**A. The Scriptures teach that sensualism, irreligious-
ness and lawlessness are to prevail generally
throughout the world in the age immediately
preceding our Lord's return.**

(1) Conditions will be the same as in the age before the
Flood, says Jesus. Matt. 24:37-39. (2) The characteristics
of the antediluvian age may be summarized as follows: (a)
religious apostasy; (b) moral degeneracy; (c) evil thinking;
(d) lawlessness; (e) sensualism; (f) preoccupation, such
that when the Flood come, it came upon an unbelieving,
unsuspecting and unprepared race; (g) vain striving of the
Holy Spirit with men. Gen. 6:1-13. (3) These conditions
are to prevail likewise in the age immediately preceding
our Lord's return. See Luke 17:26-32; 1 Tim. 4:1-3; 2 Tim.
3:1-5, etc.

161. **Q. What are to be the precursors of the Second
Coming of Christ?**

**A. The following conditions and happenings: (1)
world-wide irreligiousness and apostasy; (2)
world-wide social and political unrest; (3) the
return of the Jews to Palestine; (4) the rise
of the Antichrist.**

(1) **World-wide irreligiousness and apostasy**; i. e., a general falling away from the faith (2 Thess. 2:1-3, 1 Tim.
4:1-3, 2 Pet. 3:1-4), a corresponding moral degeneracy (2
Tim. 3:1-14, Matt. 24:37-39), and the rise of the spirit of

the antichrist (1 John 2:22, 4:3; 2 John 7). (2) **World-wide social and political unrest.** Luke 21:25-28, Matt. 24:5-8. (3) **The return of the Jews to Jerusalem and the Holy Land.** Jer. 32:36-42, Ezek. 11:16-20. Luke 21:24—"until the times of the Gentiles be fulfilled." See Rom. 11. Note, in this connection, the achievements and possibilities of the present-day Zionist Movement. (4) **The rise of the Antichrist himself**; a great world ruler or dictator, who will embody in his person and plans, intense hatred of, and opposition to, the Christian religion. See 2 Thess. 2:1-10. He will be the very embodiment of Satan in the flesh, and will be Satan's agent in a last desperate effort to defeat the execution of God's purpose and plan for the human race. (5) In addition to all this there will be **the completion of the Gospel proclamation,** so far as the present-day church order is concerned. Matt. 24:14.

162. Q. What great events are to occur in close connection with the Second Coming of Christ?

A. Apparently, the following: (1) The First Resurrection, (2) The Translation of the Church, (3) The Great Tribulation, (4) The Second Coming, (5) The Conversion of the Jews, and (6) The Millenial Reign of Christ.

(1) **The First Resurrection.** 1 Thess. 4:16, 17. Rev. 20:4-6, "they lived, and reigned with Christ a thousand years. The rest of the dead lived not until the thousand years should be finished. This is the first resurrection." In this connection, note the clear distinction running throughout the New Testament, between the "resurrection from the dead," and the "resurrection of the dead" (cf. Phil. 3:11). The former phrase, many believe, alludes to the First Resurrection (cf. John 5:29—"they that have done good, unto the resurrection of life"); and the latter phrase, to the final resurrection of all humanity, particularly the wicked and lost (cf. John 5:29—"they that have done evil, unto the

resurrection of judgment"), which will evidently follow the Millenium. Note: "the rest of the dead lived not until the thousand years should be finished" (Rev. 20:5). (2) **The Translation of the Church**, i. e., the true Bride of Christ. 1 Thess. 4:16-17. As the Jewish Dispensation came to its close with the Ascension of the Son of God; so the Christian Dispensation will end with the Ascension of the Holy Spirit and the Bride of Christ. (3) **The Great Tribulation**. Naturally the Translation of the Church will bring to an end all Gospel testimony on the earth, and as a result the Antichrist will reign supreme and unchallenged for the time being. A period of great tribulation will ensue, Matt. 24:21. This period of tribulation will culminate in world conflict, and in the last great battle of Armagedon (i. e., Megiddo, at the foot of Mount Carmel). Rev. 16:12-16. (4) **The Second Coming** will, many believe, occur in connection with this great battle. Christ will come, not **for** His saints, but **with** them, to abolish all human government and to inaugurate His millenial reign. Cf. Rev. 20:6. (5) **The Conversion of the Jews**. Christ's appearing will be so definite and undeniable, and will be accompanied by such signal manifestations of the Spirit, that the Jews will no longer reject Him. The conversion of the Jewish nation, in the main, will be the result. See Rom. 11. From that time on, through the united proclamation of the primitive Gospel by both Jews and Gentiles, the knowledge of the Lord will cover the earth as the waters cover the sea. (6) **The Millenial Reign of Christ**. It is held by many that the Second Coming will precede and usher in the Millenium. **The numerous injunctions of Christ to His people, to watch for His Second Coming, and to be ready for it at any moment, would be meaningless if that event were always a thousand years in the future**, i. e., after the Millenium. It is held, too, that Christ will reign personally; that He will sit upon the throne of David in Jerusalem (Psa. 132:11, Isa. 9:7); and that from His throne in Jerusalem

He will rule and judge the nations in righteousness. Thus the dream of the old Hebrew prophets of a Golden Age of righteousness, peace and plenty, will be realized. See Isa. 11:1-9, 35:5-10, 55:6-13, 65:17-25, etc.

163. Q. **What, then, should be the attitude of all Christians with respect to the Second Coming of Christ?**

    A. **They should desire, anticipate, pray for, watch for, and be ready at any moment for the glorious appearing of their Lord and Savior Jesus Christ.**

Mark 13:33—"Take ye heed, watch and pray. 2 Pet. 3:12 —"looking for and earnestly desiring the coming of the day of God." How unfortunate that the modern Church should have allowed this precious and great doctrine to become lost in the rubbish of materialism and religious in- difference! May the Lord hasten the day of His glorious appearing! "Come, Lord Jesus" (Rev. 22:20).

REVIEW EXAMINATION OVER LESSON FIFTY

154. Q. What do we mean by "the end of our age"?

155. Q. When will the Christian Dispensation end?

156. Q. Is the doctrine of the Second Coming of Christ prominent in the Scriptures?

157. Q. What do the Scriptures teach with respect to the nature of the Second Coming?

158. Q. What do the Scriptures teach with regard to the time of the Second Coming?

159. Q. What are to be the purposes of the Second Coming?

160. Q. What conditions are to prevail throughout the world immediately prior to the Second Coming of Christ?

161. Q. What are to be the precursors of the Second Coming of Christ?

162. Q. What great events are to occur in close connection with the Second Coming of Christ?

163. Q. What, then, should be the attitude of all Christians with respect to the Second Coming of
Christ?

Lesson Fifty-One
IMMORTALITY

Scripture Reading: 2 Cor. 5:1-10, 1 Cor. 15:35-58.

Scriptures to Memorize: "For we know that if the earthly
house of our tabernacle be dissolved, we have a building
from God, a house not made with hands, eternal in the
heavens" (2 Cor. 5:1). "But when this corruptible shall
have put on incorruption, and this mortal shall have put
on immortality, then shall come to pass the saying that is
written, Death is swallowed up in victory" (1 Cor. 15:54).

164. Q. Can we determine exactly the sequence of the
events that are to occur in the last days?

A. No; because the order of their happening is not
clearly revealed in the Scriptures.

The events themselves, as outlined in these last three lessons, are quite clearly described in the Scriptures. We cannot, however, determine the exact order of their occurrence.
To be able to do so would require that we be prophets ourselves, and would thus presuppose an inspiration we do
not claim to possess. The best we can do therefore, is to
present what appears to be their order of occurrence, in
the light of Scripture teaching.

165. Q. What events are to occur in connection with
the close of Christ's millenial reign?

A. The following, evidently: (1) The Post-millenial Apostasy; (2) The General Resurrection;

(3) The Last Judgment; (4) The Renovation of Our Earth; (5) The New Heavens and New Earth; (6) The Consummation of All Things.

(1) **The Post-millenial Apostasy,** Rev. 20:7-10; a final rebellion, incited by Satan, against the sovereignty and rule of Christ. (2) **The General Resurrection,** i. e., the resurrection of the dead. Rev. 30:5—"the rest of the dead lived not until the thousand years should be finished." Rev. 20:12—"I saw the dead, the great and the small, standing before the throne." (3) **The Last Judgment,** Acts 17:31; Matt. 12:41-42, 25:31-46; 2 Tim. 4:1; 1 Pet. 4:5; Rev. 20:11-15. (4) **The Renovation of Our Earth,** 2 Pet. 3:1-13. (5) **The New Heavens and New Earth,** Isa. 66:22-24, 2 Pet. 3:13. (6) **The Consummation of All Things,** Acts 3:20-21, 1 Cor. 15:25-28, Rev. 21:1-8 (note well: "I saw the holy city, new Jerusalem, coming down out of heaven from God;" also, "Behold, the tabernacle of God is with men"); Rev. 22:1-5.

166. Q. What is the scripture meaning of the term "resurrection"?

A. The term "resurrection" means that our bodies will be raised, and reunited with our spirits.

(1) That is, their constituent elements will be **reassembled, at least those necessary to the construction of our celestial bodies,** and will be again united with the spirit that formerly inhabited them. John 14:2—"in my Father's house are many mansions," i. e., literally, **dwelling-places, tabernacles.** Cf. 2 Cor. 5:1—"a building from God, a house not made with hands, eternal, in the heavens." Cf. also Rom. 8:11. (2) We see nothing incredible in this teaching. We must remember that **spirit** determines, unifies, vitalizes, and controls the body; not the body, the spirit. We know that in this life the spirit assembles and unifies the constituent elements of our physical bodies; therefore, we may reasonably conclude that the same spirit will have power to attract

unto itself, and unify, the elements necessary to the con'
struction of an ethereal body. 1 Cor. 15:44, 49—"if there
is a natural body, there is also a spiritual body, . . . and as
we have borne the image of the earthy, we shall also bear
the image of the heavenly." (It should be made clear at
this point, that the various scriptures quoted here have
reference only to the redeemed. Cf. Heb. 12:23—"the
spirits of just men made perfect.").

**167. Q. Do the Scriptures teach that the bodies of all
people, of all time, are to be raised up in the
last day?**

**A. The Scriptures teach that all humanity will be
raised up, to appear in the Judgment.**

(1) John 5:28, 29—"all that are in the tombs shall hear
his voice, and shall come forth," etc. Rev. 20:13—"and
the sea gave up the dead that were in it; and death and
Hades gave up the dead that were in them: and they were
judged every man according to their works." "Hades" is,
in scripture, **the unseen.** (2) All must of necessity be raised
up, in order that all may appear before the judgment'seat
of Christ. Matt. 25:31, 32—"he shall sit on the throne
of his glory, and before him shall be gathered all the na'
tions." 2 Cor. 5:10—"we must all be made manifest before
the judgment'seat of Christ." Cf. Matt. 12:41, 42; Acts
17:31; Rom. 2:16; Heb. 9:27, 28; Rev. 20:12.

**168. Q. What do the Scriptures teach regarding the
resurrection of the saints?**

**A. The Scriptures teach that the bodies of the
saints are to be resurrected and glorified.**

(1) They are to be raised **at Christ's coming.** 1 Cor. 15:22,
23—"For as in Adam all die, so also in Christ shall all be
made alive. But each in his own order: Christ the first'
fruits; then they that are Christ's **at his coming.**" See also
1 Thess. 4:16'17, Rev. 20:4'6. (2) They are to be **glorified.**
Phil. 3:20, 21—"the Lord Jesus Christ, who shall fashion

anew the body of our humiliation, that it may be conformed to the body of his glory." Dan. 12:3—"they that turn many to righteousness (shall shine) as the stars for ever and ever."

169. Q. What is the scripture meaning of the term "glorification"?

A. The term "glorification" describes the process by which the bodies of the saints shall be transformed by the working of Christ's mighty power, from mortal bodies into radiant immortal bodies.

(1) John 17:5—"Father, glorify thou me . . . with the glory which I had with thee before the world was." John 7:39—"for the Spirit was not yet given; because Jesus was not yet glorified." Rom. 8:21—"the creature itself shall also be delivered from the bondage of corruption into the liberty of the glory of the children of God." Rom. 2:7— "glory and honor and incorruption, eternal life." (2) Note, in this connection, that the body in which Jesus came forth from the tomb was the body of "flesh and bones" (i. e., evidently lacking the blood, which is the seat of animal life). It was a body in which He could pass through closed doors, i. e., it was essentially **ethereal** (Mark 16:14, Luke 24:31, John 20:19-20, 24-25). This was evidently His **resurrection body**. But the body in which He appeared to Saul of Tarsus, like that in which He was manifested on the occasion of His Transfiguration (Matt. 17:1-2), was of such radiant beauty and glory, that its brilliance outshone that of the noon-day sun (Acts 9:3-8, 22:6-9, 26:12-13). This was obviously His **heavenly** (celestial, spiritual, immortal, etc.) body. (3) 1 Cor. 15:40-44, "There are also celestial bodies, and bodies terrestrial; but the glory of the celestial is one, and the glory of the terrestrial is another. There is one glory of the sun, another glory of the moon, another glory of the stars; for one star differeth from

another star in glory. **So also is the resurrection of the dead.** It is sown in corruption, it is raised in incorruption; it is sown in dishonor, it is raised in glory; it is sown in weak‐ ness, it is raised in power; it is sown a natural body, it is raised a spiritual body. If there is a natural body, there is also a spiritual body." Cf. v. 49—"and as we have borne the image of the earthy, we shall also bear the image of the heavenly." (4) Emphasize the fact here, that through all these changes and transformations, as in the case of Je‐ sus, who was recognized by His disciples, **the individual per‐ sists.** Hence, John Smith will still be John Smith in the resurrection morning, and John Jones will still be John Jones, etc. In the processes of resurrection and glorifica‐ tion, **no loss of individual identity will occur.**

170. Q. By what phrase is this entire process of resur‐ rection and glorification described in the Scrip‐ tures?

A. It is described as the putting on of immortality. (1) 1 Cor. 15:53—"For this corruptible must put on in‐ corruption, and this mortal must put on immortality." (2) By **mortality** is meant corruption, i. e., liability to dissolu‐ tion. By **immortality** is meant incorruption, the antithesis of corruption. Rom. 2:7—"glory and honor and incorrup‐ tion." (3) The body of man, as we have learned, **was cre‐ ated mortal**; but, through the redemption which is in Christ Jesus, **it shall be made immortal**, i. e., incapable of death, dissolution, disintegration, etc. (4) In the light of these truths, it is obvious that to speak of "the immortality of the soul" is to speak unscripturally. **Immortality** is a term which pertains only to the body.

171. Q. What, then, is the scripture doctrine of immor‐ tality?

A. Immortality is the term used in scripture to describe the glory and honor and incorruption of our heavenly bodies.

Hence it is said of Christ, the firstborn from the dead, that He "only hath immortality" (1 Tim. 6:16). The resurrection, ascension and glorification of Christ are God's evidences, likewise His solemn pledges, to all mankind, that His saints shall all, in like manner, ultimately be raised up and clothed in the same glory and honor and incorruption. See 1 John 3:2, 1 Pet. 1:3-5.

172. Q. But: How are those saints who may be living on the earth when Christ comes again, to come into possession of their immortal bodies?

A. The Scriptures teach that they are to put on immortality by transfiguration and glorification.

1 Cor. 15:51, 52—"Behold, I tell you a mystery; we shall not all sleep, but we shall all be changed" (i. e., we who are living upon the earth when Jesus comes again); "in a moment, in the twinkling of an eye, at the last trump; for the trumpet shall sound, and the dead shall be raised incorruptible, and we shall be changed" (i. e., we who are still in the flesh shall be transfigured). 1 Thess. 4:16-17—"For the Lord Himself shall descend from heaven, with a shout, with the voice of the archangel, and with the trump of God; and the dead in Christ shall rise first; then we that are alive, that are left, shall together with them be caught up in the clouds, to meet the Lord in the air; and so shall we ever be with the Lord." 1 Cor. 15:53, 54—"For this corruptible must put on incorruption, and this mortal must put on immortality. But when this corruptible (the saints whose bodies are in the grave) shall have put on incorruption (by resurrection and glorification), and this mortal (the saints who are alive and remain unto the coming of the Lord) shall have put on immortality (by transfiguration and glorification); then shall come to pass the saying that is written, Death is swallowed up in victory!" This entire section of the Scriptures is descriptive of the Translation of the Church.

173. Q. What, then, are the two phases of Christ's redemptive work?

A. They are: (1) the present redemption of our spirits from the guilt of sin; and (2) the final redemption of our bodies from the consequences of sin.

(1) Gal. 3:13—"Christ redeemed us from the curse of the law," i. e., from the guilt and penalty of sin. Eph. 1:7—"in whom we have our redemption through his blood." (2) Rom. 8:23—"waiting for our adoption, to wit, the redemption of our body." Thus the redemption that is in Christ Jesus includes, ultimately, **our redemption from mortality itself,** as well as redemption from suffering, disease, and death. 2 Cor. 5:4—"that what is mortal may be swallowed up of life." (3) No cripples in heaven, then; no deformity, disease, suffering, death, etc. Rev. 21:4—"God shall wipe away every tear from their eyes; and death shall be no more; neither shall there be mourning, nor crying, nor pain, any more: the first things are passed away." Rom. 8:21—"the creation itself also shall be delivered from the bondage of corruption into the liberty of the glory of the children of God." (4) Our race started out on this earth **innocent** and **mortal**; the redeemed race, in the new heavens and new earth, will be **holy** and **immortal.**

174. Q. In what is the superlative excellence of the Christian Religion manifested?

A. It is manifested in this blessed promise and glorious hope of the redemption of our bodies.

No other system of either philosophy or religion holds out such a precious promise, such a glorious hope, such a powerful incentive to righteousness and holiness on our part! In view of all these great truths, "what manner of persons ought ye to be in all holy living and godliness, looking for and earnestly desiring the coming of the day of God!" (2 Pet. 3:11-12).

REVIEW EXAMINATION OVER LESSON
FIFTY-ONE

164. Q. Can we determine exactly the sequence of the events that are to occur in the last days?

165. Q. What events are to occur in connection with the close of Christ's millenial reign?

166. Q. What is the scripture meaning of the term "resurrection"?

167. Q. Do the Scriptures teach that the bodies of all people, of all time, are to be raised up in the last day?

168. Q. What do the Scriptures teach regarding the resurrection of the saints?

169. Q. What is the scripture meaning of the term "glorification"?

170. Q. By what phrase is this entire process of resurrection and glorification described in the Scriptures?

171. Q. What, then, is the scripture doctrine of immortality?

172. Q. But: How are those saints who may be living on the earth when Christ comes again, to come into possession of their immortal bodies?

173. Q. What, then, are the two phases of Christ's redemptive work?

174. Q. In what is the superlative excellence of the Christian Religion manifested?

Lesson Fifty-Two
THE GLORIOUS CONSUMMATION

Scripture Reading: 1 Cor. 15:20-28, 2 Pet. 3:1-13, Rev. 21:1-8, 22:1-5.

Scriptures to Memorize: "Then cometh the end, when he shall deliver up the kingdom to God, even the Father, when he shall have abolished all rule and all authority and power" (1 Cor. 15:24). "But, according to his promise, we look for new heavens and a new earth, wherein dwelleth righteousness" (2 Pet. 3:13).

---

175.   Q.   What, according to the Scriptures, is to be the disposition of the bodies of all those who are lost?

A.   The Scriptures teach that the bodies of the lost are to be raised up and reunited with their spirits, but not glorified.

(1) 1 Cor. 15:22—"For as in Adam all die, so also in Christ shall all be made alive." John 5:28, 29—"all that are in the tombs shall hear his voice, and shall come forth: they that have done good, unto the resurrection of life: and they that have done evil, unto the resurrection of judgment." Rev. 20:13—"And the sea gave up the dead that were in it; and death and Hades (the grave) gave up the dead that were in them: and they were judged every man according to their works." (2) This general resurrection of the dead is obviously to occur at the close of Christ's millenial reign. Rev. 20:5—"the rest of the dead lived not until the thousand years should be finished."

176.   Q.   For what event is this general resurrection of the dead to be a preparation?

A.   It is to be a preparation for the Last Judgment.

The Scriptures teach that the Last Judgment is (1) something to be expected in the future (Acts 24:25, Heb.

10:27); (2) something that is to follow death (Heb. 9:27); (3) something that is to be attended by all humanity (Matt. 12:41-42, Acts 17:31, Matt. 16:27, 2 Cor. 5:10, Matt. 25:31-32); (4) something for which those who are evil are "reserved" (2 Pet. 2:4, 9; Matt. 13:24-30, 36-43); (5) something for which the resurrection of the dead is a preparation (John 5:29, Rev. 20:11-15).

177. Q. What is the Last Judgment?

 A. It is to be that event in which all humanity will, with all the angels, be assembled before God in the person of Christ, for a final reckoning.

See Acts 17:31, Matt. 25:31-46; Rev. 20:11-15.

178. Q. Who will be the Judge in the Last Judgment?

 A. The Scriptures teach that Christ will be the Judge.

(1) Though God is the Judge of all (Heb. 12:23), yet His judicial activity is exercised through Christ, both in the present state and at the last day. John 5:22—"for neither doth the Father judge any man, but he hath given all judgment unto the Son." Cf. Matt. 19:28, 25:31-32; Acts 17:31; 2 Cor. 5:10; Rev. 3:21. (2) Christ will appear in the Judgment in His threefold official capacity. As Prophet, He will reveal the Father to His saints in glory (John 16:25, 17:24-26). As Priest, He will present His saints before the Throne as an elect race, a redeemed people, a purchased possession (1 Pet. 2:9). As King, He will judge the world in righteousness (Acts 17:31).

179. Q. Who are to be the subjects of the Last Judgment?

 A. Two classes: (1) the entire human race, and (2) the evil angels.

(1) All humanity, each person possessed of body reunited with spirit, the dead having been raised, and the living hav-

ing been changed. 1 Thess. 4:16-17; 1 Cor. 15:51-52; Matt. 25:31-33; Rev. 20:12-13. (2) **The evil angels** (2 Pet. 2:4, Jude 6); the good angels appearing only as attendants and ministers of the righteous Judge (Matt. 13:39-42, 24:31; Matt. 25:31; 2 Thess. 1:7-10).

180. Q. What will be the grounds of the final judgment?

A. They will be two in number: (1) the grace of Christ, and (2) the law of God.

(1) Rev. 20:12. Those whose names are "written in the book of life" are to be found approved on the ground of their union with Christ and participation in His righteousness. They will be presented in the Judgment clothed in glory and honor and immortality. (2) Those whose names are not "written in the book of life" will be judged by the law of God, as it was revealed in the particular dispensation under which they lived. For instance, those who lived under the law of Moses, will be judged by that law; and those who live under the Gospel, the law of the Spirit, are to be judged by the law of the Spirit, etc. Heathen nations that had no revealed law on earth, are to be judged by their respective moral codes (i. e., existing in the form of tradition). Rom. 2:12-16.

181. Q. What is to be the nature of the Last Judgment?

A. It will be "the revelation of the righteous judgment of God."

(1) Not the ascertainment of the moral character of those appearing for judgment, but the revelation of God's righteousness, justice, and holiness. The idea that God will line all men up in a row and look them over, to ascertain their moral standing, is absurd. Our moral standing is known to God fully every moment of our lives. (2) Judgment will be, rather, the "revelation of the righteous judgment of God" (Rom. 2:5-6), to all intelligent creatures, both angels and men. (3) Thus the saints will be presented in the

Judgment clad in the fine linen of righteousness (Rev. 19:8, 14), their sins having been covered by the atoning blood of Christ, forgiven and forgotten, put away from them forever; and clothed also in glory and honor and immortality, the habiliments of eternal redemption. **In their manifestation, the greatness of God's love, mercy and salvation will be fully disclosed to all His creatures.** (4) The wicked will be presented in the Judgment **as they really are,** i. e., in all the realism of their rebelliousness, neglect and iniquity. Even their secret sins will be brought to light and revealed to the whole intelligent creation. For the first time perhaps, they will thus be made to realize the enormity of their sin, and the corresponding awfulness of their loss of God and heaven; and the result indeed will be weeping and wailing and gnashing of teeth (i. e., not of hate, but of **remorse** and **despair**). (5) This final demonstration will be sufficient to prove to all intelligent creatures that Satan's charges against God have, from the beginning, been false and malicious. **The result will be the complete vindication of God Almighty, which is, in itself, the primary design of the Last Judgment.** Cf. 1 Cor. 6:2, 3—"know ye not that the saints shall judge the world? ... know ye not that we shall judge angels?" This final demonstration of God's matchless love, in the salvation of His saints, will be sufficient of itself to condemn Satan and his rebel hosts forever. (6) This demonstration will also be sufficient to deter the saints from ever lapsing a second time into apostasy and sin; and thus the possibility of sin in the future state will have been entirely eradicated.

182.   Q.   What is to follow the Last Judgment?

A.   The Scriptures teach that, following the Judgment, both the saved and the lost will enter upon their respective eternal states of being.

Matt. 26:34, 41—"Then shall the King say unto them on his right hand, Come, ye blessed of my Father, inherit the kingdom prepared for you from the foundation of the world ... Then shall he say also unto them on the left hand, Depart from me, ye cursed, into the eternal fire which is prepared for the devil and his angels." John 5:29—"they that have done good, unto the resurrection of life; and they that have done evil, unto the resurrection of judgment" (literally, **condemnation**).

183. Q. **What is to be the essential characteristic of the eternal state of the righteous?**

A. **It is to be essentially a state of personal union and communion with God.**

It is also described as **eternal life** (Matt. 25:46); **rest** (Heb. 4:9), i. e., release from earthly afflictions and trials; **spiritual society** (Heb. 12:23); **communion with God** (Rev. 21:3); **worship** (Rev. 19:1); **glory and honor and incorruption** (Rom. 2:7); and **perfect holiness** (Rev. 21:27).

184. Q. **What is to be the essential characteristic of the eternal state of the lost?**

A. **It is to be essentially a state of separation from God and from the society of the redeemed.**

It is described under such phrases and terms as: **eternal fire** (Matt. 25:41); **the outer darkness** (Matt. 8:12); **weeping and the gnashing of teeth** (Matt. 8:12); **the pit of the abyss** (Rev. 9:2, 11); **eternal punishment** (Matt. 25:46); **torment** (Rev. 14:10, 11); **wrath of God** (Rom. 2:5); **eternal sin** (Mark 3:29); **second death** (Rev. 21:8); and "**eternal destruction from the face of the Lord and from the glory of his might**" (2 Thess. 1:9). Obviously its essential characteristics are to be **remorse, despair,** and **hopelessness.**

185. Q. **What, then, is hell, according to the teaching of the Scriptures?**

A. **Hell is the penitentiary of the moral universe in which all the wicked will, with the devil and his angels, be segregated forever.**

(1) For the Scripture doctrine of hell (literally, **Gehenna**), see Matt. 5:22, 29; 10:28, 18:9, 23:33; Mark 9:43-47; Luke 12:5; Jas. 3:6; Rev. 20:14-15, 21:8, etc. (2) Hell has been prepared for the devil and his angels (Matt. 25:41). Wicked men will eventually go to hell, not because God will cast them into it, but because their own consciences will drive them, instinctively, to their proper place, as in the case of Judas (Acts 2:25). As water seeks its own level, they who in this present life fit themselves only for the society of the rebellious, wicked and unbelieving, will instinctively seek that type of society in the next world. For, without doubt, the devil and all his kind would be miserable in heaven. (3) "Sin is self-isolating, unsocial, selfish. By virtue of natural laws the sinner reaps as he has sown, and sooner or later is repaid by desertion or contempt. Then the selfishness of one sinner is punished by the selfishness of another, the ambition of one by the ambition of another, the cruelty of one by the cruelty of another. The misery of the wicked hereafter will doubtless be due in part to the spirit of their companions. They dislike the good, whose presence and example is a continual reproof and reminder of the height from which they have fallen, and they shut themselves out of their company. The Judgment will bring about a complete cessation of intercourse between the good and the bad" (Strong, **Systematic Theology**, p. 1035). Cf. Rev. 22:11-12. A truly asinine notion is explicit in the claim one hears so often in our day that New Testament passages alluding to hell (and to heaven, as well) are "merely figurative." This claim ignores the evident fact that a figure, in order to be a figure, must be a figure **of something** (just as a symbol is a symbol of something, a proposition is an affirmation or denial about something, a sentence is a predication about something, etc.): in short, without the genuine, the counterfeit is impossible. (Indeed, in the Platonic dialogues, the **mythos** is poetic imagery to which men must resort, because of the inadequacy of language, to reveal

profound truth which cannot be set forth in propositional terms. It is the device, according to Plato, which men are compelled to use to communicate the **ineffable**. Cf. Rom. 8:26-27). Hence, if Scripture passages which describe hell as "eternal fire," "the lake that burneth with fire and brimstone," "outer darkness," "the bottomless pit" ("abyss"), etc., are figurative, I shudder to think what the reality (the separation of the soul from all Good) is. To try to pass off these expressions as "figurative" is not to "explain them away," — it is to multiply the problem a hundredfold. Need we be reminded of the awful internal pain of mental anguish. Perhaps conscience will turn out to be the fire that is never quenched and memory the worm that never dies. See Luke 16:19-31, Rev. 6:15-17; Heb. 10:31, 2 Cor. 5:11, Gen. 28:16-17, Mark 9:43-48, etc.

186. Q. **What is to be "the consummation of all things"?**

A. **The "consummation of all things" evidently will include: (1) the renovation of our earth by fire; (2) the establishment of new heavens and a new earth; and (3) the return of Christ's authority to the Father, that God may be all in all.**

See Acts 3:20-21, 2 Pet. 3:1-13, 1 Cor. 15:24-28, Rev. 21:1-8, Rev. 22:1-5.

187. Q. **By what criterion will the success of God's Plan of the Universe be evaluated, in the finality of things?**

A. **It will be evaluated, not by the number who are saved, but by the greatness of the salvation that God will ultimately reveal in His saints.**

A holy redeemed race! The consummation and realization of His eternal purpose and plan! "O the depth of the riches both of the wisdom and the knowledge of God!" Praise His holy name forever!

REVIEW EXAMINATION OVER LESSON
FIFTY-TWO

175. Q.   What, according to the Scriptures, is to be the disposition of the bodies of all those who are lost?

176. Q.   For what event is this general resurrection of the dead to be a preparation?

177. Q.   What is the Last Judgment?

178. Q.   Who will be the Judge in the Last Judgment?

179. Q.   Who are to be the subjects of the Last Judgment?

180. Q.   What will be the grounds of the final judgment?

181. Q.   What is to be the nature of the Last Judgment?

182. Q.   What is to follow the Last Judgment?

183. Q.   What is to be the essential characteristic of the eternal state of the righteous?

184. Q.   What is to be the essential characteristic of the eternal state of the lost?

185. Q.   What, then, is hell, according to the teaching of the Scriptures?

186. Q.   What is to be "the consummation of all things"?

187. Q.   By what criterion will the success of God's Plan of the Universe be evaluated, in the finality of things?

SPECIAL STUDY: ON CONVERSION, AS SHOWN BY REPRESENTATIVE CASES IN ACTS

S.M.—special mention.   N.I.—necessary inference.
F.I.—fair inference

It should be noted that special mention is made of preaching or hearing as the **beginning**, and of baptism as the end of the process.

	Preaching and/or Hearing	Faith	Repentance	Confession	Baptism	Rejoicing
Acts II Pentecost—Three Thousand	S.M. 2:4, 2:14-37	N.I. 2:37,41	S.M. 2:38	F.I. (cf. Matt. 10:32-33)	S.M. 2:38	S.M. 2:46,47
Acts VIII Samaritans	S.M. 8:5-6	S.M. 8:12	F.I.	F.I.	S.M. 8:12,13	S.M. 8:8
Acts VIII The Eunuch	S.M. 8:35	S.M. 8:37 ? (A.V.)	F.I.	S.M. 8:37 ? (A.V.)	S.M. 8:36-39	S.M. 8:39
Acts IX, XXII, XXVI Saul of Tarsus	S.M. 9:5-6, 17-18; 22:12-15; 26:12-18	N.I. 9:6; 22:10; 26:19	N.I. 9:8-11	N.I. 9:5; 22:10	S.M. 9:18; 22:16; Rom. 6:3-5	N.I. 9:18; 26:19
Acts X, XI, XV Cornelius	S.M. 10:6, 34-43; 11:13-15; 15:7-9	N.I. 10:46; 15:7-9	F.I.	F.I.	S.M. 10:47,48	S.M. 10:46-48
Acts XVI Lydia	S.M. 16:13	S.M. 16:14	F.I.	F.I.	S.M. 16:15	S.M. 16:15,40
Acts XVI The Jailor	S.M. 16:32	N.I. 16:31,34	F.I.	F.I.	S.M. 16:33	S.M. 16:34
Acts XVIII Corinthians	S.M. 18:4,5	S.M. 18:8	F.I.	F.I.	S.M. 18:8	F.I.

*This material follows partially the diagram which may be found in the book, **Pulpit Diagrams**, by the late Z. T. Eweeney.

In summarizing the content of the accompanying diagram, the following matters of fact should be noted especially:

1. That there are eight specific cases of conversion to Christ reported in the book of Acts. Of course, there are cases of non-conversion also: notably, the Jewish ecclesiastics who rejected Stephen's testimony; the Athenian philosophers on Mars Hill; Felix, Festus, and Agrippa (chs. 7, 17, 24, 25, 26). The Gospel is the power of God unto salvation only to those who believe (John 1:12-13, Luke 8:14-15, Rom. 1:16); to those who reject it, it becomes the power of God unto damnation (2 Cor. 2:15-16, John 3:17-18, 5:28-29, Rom. 2:4-11, etc.).

2. That in every case of conversion reported, specific mention is made of **preaching** and/or **hearing** as the initial step, and of **baptism** as the consummating act of the process.

3. That in all cases, sinners who asked what to do, were told what to do, and did what they were told to do, without delay, and then the Lord added them to His Body (Acts 2:47). There was no praying, agonizing, or waiting for a "special experience" (the visitation of an angel, a voice "from heaven," the singing of a choir invisible, a portent in the sky, an unexplainable ecstasy, or what not) as evidence of a miraculous "call"; the "mourners' bench" had not yet been built by theological carpentry. All this came in later with human "theology." There was no catechism, no "confirmation," no voting on the fitness of sinners for admission into the local church. On the contrary, everything was extreme simplicity. Moreover, all who were added to the church, came into covenant relationship with God through Christ in precisely the same way on precisely the same terms.

4. That in the instances in which rejoicing is mentioned, the rejoicing is reported as following baptism. The only (partial) exception to this principle may be found in Acts 8:8; here the healings wrought by Philip the evangelist

contributed to the general rejoicing when the Gospel was first brought to the Samaritans.

5.   That in some of these cases reported, no mention is made of **repentance**. Repentance is, of course, a turning to God in disposition and will, a turning that will manifest itself in a new life (Luke 3:7-14). It seems obvious that such a change was not needed in such cases as those of the Ethiopian eunuch (Acts 8:26-40), Cornelius and his house (Acts 10:1-22), Lydia and her helpers (Acts 16:11, 15). (See, in this connection, Luke 15:7 especially.) These persons were already turned to God in will and life, to the extent of their knowledge; hence, what they needed was additional light, sufficient to make them Christians, and when that light was shed upon them, they proceeded to obey the Gospel at once (Acts 8:36, 10:33, 16:14). In the case of the Philippian jailor, his every act, after hearing the Word, evinced a complete change of heart and of directionality of life, that is to say, a genuine repentance (Acts 16:27-34).

6.   What must one do to be saved?—in the light of this clear New Testament teaching? The answers may be cited as follows: (1) to the non-believer, like the Philippian jailor, only a general command could be given, awaiting further necessary edification (Acts 16:31-34); (2) to the believer, like the three thousand on the Day of Pentecost (Acts 2:38); (3) to the penitent believer, as Saul of Tarsus was (Acts 22:16, cf. Acts 9:9); (4) to the baptized penitent believer, the Christian (Phil. 2:12, 1 Pet. 1:5-11, Acts 2:42, 1 Cor. 15:58, etc.); (5) to the backslider, as was Simon the sorcerer (Acts 8:22; cf. 1 John 1:9). Thus it will be seen that the answer was tailored, so to speak, to the inquirer's spiritual status — the point to which he had already advanced in the process of conversion — at the time he propounded the question. Rom. 10:10—"with the heart man believeth unto righteousness." 2 Cor. 7:10—

"godly sorrow worketh repentance unto salvation." Rom. 10:10—"with the mouth confession is made unto salva' tion." Gal. 3:27—"for as many of you as were baptized into Christ did put on Christ."

SPECIAL STUDY: ON "MILLENIALISM"

I should like to add a word of caution here on the general subject of "Millenialism."

1. That our Lord is coming again is emphasized on page after page of the New Testament. In fact, there are as many Scriptures in the New Testament writings pointing forward to the Lord's second advent as there are Scriptures in the Old Testament pointing forward to the facts of His first coming and His ministry in the flesh. And it is signi' ficant, I think, that the passages alluding to the Second Coming are as generally ignored by professing Christians of our time as those of the Old Testament alluding to His first coming were ignored — and ultimately repudiated — by His people of the Old Covenant.

2. The notion that the Second Coming will take place, not as a personal manifestation of Messiah, but through the gradual world-wide acceptance of the Gospel, has not an iota of Scripture evidence to support it. In fact, Scrip' ture teaching is all to the contrary. Jesus Himself tells us that the Gospel can bring forth the fruit of the Spirit only when it is received into honest and good hearts (Luke 8:4-15, the Parable of the Soils, not the "Parable of the Sower"); and the Apostle declares it to be the power of God unto salvation to one class only, namely, to those who believe, that is, to those who accept, obey, and live it (Rom. 1:16). "Post-millenialism" of this kind is absurd, on the face of it.

3. "Millenial" theories are at best more or less specula' tive, and can hardly be otherwise. The concept is based

on the twentieth chapter of the book of Revelation. The word "millenium" is derived from the Latin indeclinable adjective, **mille**, meaning "a thousand" (Greek, **chilia**). The fact that the time element apparently is never rigid in the Plan of God (nor in the operations of the Spirit of God) should cause us to refrain from dogmatism with respect to the sequence of events connected in Scripture teaching with the Second Coming: "a thousand years" may simply designate a period of indefinite duration: cf. 2 Pet. 3:8. "Time-setting" has been discredited uniformly throughout the history of Christianity; hence, to indulge in such an absurd practice, especially since Jesus Himself has stated expressly that no one but the Heavenly Father knows when the Second Advent will occur (Matt. 24:36, Mark 13:32- 37, Acts 1:7), surely is a mark either of ignorance or of sheer presumption.

4. Of course, as stated above, Christ's numerous injunc- tions to His disciples, to watch for His Second Coming, and to be ready for it at any moment, would be meaningless if that event were always a thousand years in the future, that is, after the Millenium (post-millenial). Cf. Mark 13:33-37, Matt. 24:42-44, 2 Pet. 3:12, 1 Cor. 1:7, Rom. 8:19-23, etc.

5. Any theory that would have us believe that Jesus will not set up His Kingdom until He comes the second time is disproved (1) by the numerous passages in the New Testament which clearly indicate that the Kingdom—Mes- siah's Reign—was ushered in on the Day of Pentecost with the first proclamation of the facts of the Gospel **as facts** (Acts 2) and the subsequent incorporation of the Body of Christ (Acts 2:41, 47), and (2) by those passages which explicitly identify obedient believers in the apostolic age as being both members of the Church and citizens of the Kingdom. The Son of God assumed the Kingship (Sover- eignty after His conquest of death (on earth He had been the Uncrowned King); the ten days between His Ascen-

sion and the Advent of the Spirit on Pentecost obviously were the days of His Coronation in Heaven (Ps. 24:7-10).

It was at this time that God the Father, through the agency of the Spirit, raised Him from the dead (Rom. 8:11), seated Him at His (the Father's) own right hand in the heavenly places, and vested Him with the scepter of the Kingdom, crowned Him King of kings and Lord of lords (John 17:5, Acts 1:9-11; Eph. 1:20-23, 4:8; Heb. 1:1-4; Phil. 2:9-11; 1 Pet. 3:21-22; Acts 7:56; 1 Tim. 6:13-16; 1 Pet. 3:21-22; Rev. 1:17-18, etc.). Note especially the following passages which affirm, either implicitly or explicitly, the concurrent existence of the Kingdom with that of the present (Christian) Dispensation: Matt. 3:2—"the kingdom of heaven is at hand." Luke 10:9—"the kingdom of God is come nigh unto you." Luke 17:21—"the kingdom of God is within you." Matt. 6:33—"Seek ye first his kingdom, and his righteousness," etc. . Acts 8:12—"but when they believed Philip preaching good tidings concerning the kingdom of God and the name of Jesus Christ," etc. Col. 1:13—"the Father . . . who delivered us out of the power of darkness into the kingdom of the Son of his love," etc. See also Rev. 1:9; Acts 1:1-3, 19:8, 28:23, 31; especially 1 Cor. 15:20-28; Dan. 7:13, 14, 27; Heb. 12:28; Matt. 24:14; Luke 19:12; also the many scriptures in which the rise and spread of the Kingdom is described, usually in parable, e.g., Matt. 13:18-52, Mark 4:26-32, Luke 13:18-21, etc. See also Matt. 16:15-20 (in this passage, "my church" and "the keys of the kingdom of heaven" are clearly correlative); 1 Thess. 2:12, 2 Pet. 1:11, 2 Tim. 4:1, etc. This Kingdom is eternal, of course, by virtue of the fact that its locale is the interior life of the redeemed; hence it is said that their citizenship is in heaven (Phil. 3:20), that is, their names are recorded in the Lamb's Book of Life (Rev. 21:27, 3:5).

Incidentally, those who reject the petition, "Thy kingdom

come," as included in what is commonly designated the Lord's Prayer (Matt. 6:10), on the ground that the Kingdom did come on Pentecost (Acts 2), have missed the intent of this petition. The Lord means for us to pray — so it seems to me — not just "Thy kingdom come," but, literally, "let come thy kingdom, let be done thy will, as in heaven, so also upon the earth." This is a prayer that the Kingdom may be extended throughout the whole wide world, and is a reminder to all Christians that the fulfilment of this petition is dependent on the world-wide proclamation of the Gospel (Matt. 24:14). To be sure, the Kingdom "came" in heaven fully, with the expulsion of Satan and his rebel hosts (Luke 10:18, 2 Pet. 2:4, Jude 6), and as the Reign of the Messiah it "came" on earth with the first proclamation of the Gospel. But its full "coming" on earth will depend on the fidelity of the Church to its two fold mission, that of preserving the truth of God and proclaiming it "unto the uttermost part of the earth" (Matt. 28:18-20, Luke 24:45-49, Acts 1:8).

The Kingdom may be more comprehensive than the Church in that it may—and surely does—include the innocent and the irresponsible (babies and small children, Mark 10:14, Luke 18:16) and probably the elect of former Dispensations (Eph. 4:8, Heb. 9:23-28). Nevertheless to be in the Church is to be in the Kingdom according to New Testament teaching.

It could turn out, I should think, that a personal reign of Christ upon earth, if such is indicated by the "millenial" passages in Revelation, would be, first of all, for the purpose of destroying all civil governments and instituting in their stead a universal theocracy; that this would be preparatory to the ultimate "time of restoration of all things, whereof God spake by he mouth of his holy prophets that have been from of old" (Acts 3:21; cf. Isa. 65:17, 66:22-24; Heb. 12:26-27; 2 Pet. 3:13; Rev. 21:1). Under this view the personal reign of Christ would become simply the climactic phase of the history of the Kingdom on earth (Isa. 45:5-7, 18-19, 22-25; Isa. 46:9-11).

Of course, there are many eminent loyal Biblical scholars who reject in toto the concept of a personal reign of Christ on earth. In a booklet written and published by A. C. Williams and J. H. Dykes (which may be procured from Harding College, Searcy, Arkansas), I find the following:

SEVEN OBJECTIONS TO PROMILLENIALISM'S EARTHLY REIGN: 1. The everlasting kingdom rules out the temporal world (Isa. 9:6-7). 2. Jesus' refusal of an earthly kingdom once proves he would not want one now or later (John 6:15). 3. Simultaneous kingship and priesthood are not possible on earth (Heb. 8:4). 4. Heavenly citizenship precludes any idea of an earthly kingdom (Phil. 3:20). 5. A heavenly message excludes an earthly law (Heb. 12:25). 6. Kings do not sit on footstools, but on thrones (Isa. 66:1). 7. It would: A. "Bring Christ down" (Rom. 10:6). B. Bring the law back and substitute it for the gospel (Jude 3, Gal. 5:4). C. Substitute animal sacrifice for Christ's blood (1 Pet. 1:19). D. Substitute force for free will (Rev. 22:17). E. Substitute carnal weapons for spiritual weapons (2 Cor. 10:4). F. Substitute a perishing, reeling, rocking earth for the immovable, heavenly, eternal home. G. Substitute sight for faith (2 Cor. 5:7).

PREMILLENIALISM'S NULLIFICATION ORDINANCE: 1. It nullifies the plan God made to save men. 2. It nullifies the sacrifice Jesus made for man. 3. It nullifies the gospel given to teach men. 4. It nullifies finality of God's offer to men. 5. It nullifies Jesus' present power over men. 6. It nullifies "the eternal purpose" that the church should rescue men. 7. It nullifies the great commission offered to all men.

SEVEN MISTAKES OF PREMILLENIALISTS:

1. They separate the church and the kingdom (Matt. 16:18. 2. They confuse the coming of an angel with the return of Christ (Rev. 20:1). 3. They literalize Bible symbols and thus destroy symbolic beauty and significance. 4. They offer a fleshly, earthly program and reign for fleshly-minded people (John 18:36). 5. They set their affections on things of earth instead of heaven (Col. 3:2). 6. They aspire to rule over their fellows. 7. They divide the church over their wild speculations.

I must confess to being unable to convince myself that the inferences which are drawn, in the foregoing excerpt, from the corresponding Scriptures cited, are, as a rule, necessary inferences. For example, the statement, "the everlasting kingdom rules out the temporal world." This is not necessarily true, any more than it is not true that, at any time, the fact that part of God's family is in heaven rules out the possibility that another part is on earth (cf. Eph. 3:15, Phil. 3:20, Heb. 12:22, etc.). Again, we are told that "simultaneous kingship and priesthood are not possible on earth," and the Scripture warrant cited for this view is Hebrews 8:4. But the passage cited has reference solely to the Levitical priesthood which Jesus could not exercise because He hailed from the tribe of Judah. We know, as a matter of fact, that while He was in the flesh, He frequently exercised the prerogatives of both king (though an uncrowned king, to be sure) and priest by granting forgiveness of sins (Matt. 9:1-7, Mark 2:1-11, Luke 7:44-50, etc.). As a matter of fact, too, His kingship and priesthood have existed from eternity in God's eternal purpose (Ps. 110); hence His priesthood is said to be after the order of Melchizedek, that is, not by the authority of a carnal commandment (fleshly descent) but by the power of an endless life (Heb. 7:1-17). As far as this writer is con-cerned, a dogmatic anti-premillenialism is just as repugnant as a dogmatic pro-premillenialism. This is an area of Bibli-cal exegesis in which dogmatism is not warranted, especially not to the extent of making any particular theory of the sequence of "final things," either overtly or **sub rosa** a test of fellowship in a church of the New Testament order.

To be sure, there are many eminent Bible scholars who reject **in toto** the concept of a future personal Messianic reign on earth, largely on the following grounds: 1. That the passages in the twentieth chapter of the Apocalypse on which the "millenial" doctrines are based, do not neces-sarily indicate that this will be an earthly reign; that, on the contrary, it probably indicates a mystical reign of the Christian martyrs with Christ in heaven. (Some say that these passages point to a reign of Christ in the hearts and lives of His saints on earth, a reign in which the spirit of the martyrs will be revived and will reanimate the Church on earth.) 2. That the doctrine of the "first resurrection" is being fulfilled in the conversion of sinners to Christ throughout the present Dispensation, or will be fulfilled in the envisioned great moral and spiritual resurrection that will, it is held, usher in the Millenium, that is, as the final reign of Christ in the lives of His saints on earth. (I find it difficult to harmonize this view with the Apostle's teach-ing in 1 Thess. 4:13-17, 1 Cor. 15:50-55, etc.) 3. That the term "millenium," from "mille," as stated above, is to be understood as indicating "a round period of great dura-tion." (Probably true; cf. 2 Pet. 3:8.) 4. That statements regarding the ultimate restoration of the Jews have refer-ence not to their re-establishment of an earthly (quasi-theocratic) order in Palestine, but to their conversion to Christ and induction, on the same terms as Gentiles, into the New Covenant. Hence, the phrase, "all Israel," in Paul's affirmation that eventually, after "the fulness of the

Gentiles be come in, all Israel shall be saved," is said to designate "spiritual Israel," that is, the Body of Christ made up of both Gentiles and Jews (Rom. 11:25-32; cf. Eph. 2:11-18, Gal. 3:27-29, 1 Cor. 12:13, etc.). (The "all," as used here, means, says Lard, **Commentary on Romans,** p. 370, "a very great number.")

Milligan, on the other hand, **Scheme of Redemption,** pp. 536-577, takes the position that the beginning of the end of the present Dispensation will occur with the return of the Jews to their geographical homeland, under the guardianship of the archangel Michael (Exo. 23:20-25, 32:34; Num. 20:16; Josh. 5:13-15; Isa. 43:9; Dan. 10:13, 21; 12:1-3). He lists what he believes to be the sequence of events leading to the Consummation of all things, as follows: 1. Fall of the Turkish or Ottoman Empire. 2. Reallotment of Palestine. 3. Return of the Israelites to Palestine from all parts of the world. That this return is the "restoration" that is to take place in fulfillment of Daniel 12:2-3, Milligan contends, because in the final and literal resurrection the bodies of **all** will be raised (John 5:28-29), whereas in the case to which the angel refers here only **many** of them "that sleep in the dust" shall awake. He bases his case also on other passages, such as a comparison of Dan. 10:14 and 12:3 (here we are told that some of these Israelites will, after their own "resurrection," turn many to righteousness, whereas after the literal resurrection of the dead, there will be no more preaching, hence no more conversions); also 1 Thess. 4:15-17, 2 Thess. 1:6-10; Ezek. chs. 36, 37, 39; Isa. 11:10-12, Jer. 23:3-8, etc. 4. The purpose of many nations to dispossess the restored Israelites (Rev. 16:13-14; cf. chapters 36 and 37 of Ezekiel). 5. The utter overthrow of these hostile powers in the battle of Harmageddon (Rev. 16:16), resulting in the general conversion of the Israelites (cf. Ezek. 39:22, the third chapter of Joel, the twelfth chapter of Zechariah, also Rom. 11:11-

32). 6. Destruction of all anti-Christian powers and combinations. (Milligan names "Popery, Mahometanism, and other anti-Christian powers and combinations." Present-day conditions, it seems to me, would point to Atheistic Leninism, Oriental paganism, and Mohammedanism, as corresponding, respectively to the Beast, the Dragon, and the False Prophet. The totalitarian godless state is the very essence of diabolism.) 7. Conversion of the world by the Israelites. (Dan. 10:14, 12:3; Rom. 11:12-15). This will be the great age of Gospel preaching, Milligan thinks, in which Jew and Gentile will unite to proclaim primitive Christianity throughout the whole world, and hence will bring in 8. The Millenial reign of the saints, toward the end of which there will be 9. A post-millenial apostasy, and 10. The second personal coming of Christ, and the Last Judgment.

So much for Milligan's theory. Moses E. Lard (**Commentary on Romans**, p. 359) states the theory by which "restored Israel" is identified with "spiritual Israel," as follows, commenting on Paul's language in the eleventh chapter of Romans:

> . . . the future reception of the Jews will not consist in restoring them, as Jews, to their former national prosperity, but in receiving them into the divine favor in virtue of their obedience to Christ. Their condition and state will then be precisely the same as the present condition and state of Christian Gentiles. Between the two peoples, no distinctions can exist. . . . the Gentiles are now in countless numbers dead in sin, dead to righteousness, dead to Christ. Their more general regeneration will certainly be life from the dead. Besides, when the Jews accept Christ and devote themselves wholly to preaching the gospel, I look for the scenes of the primitive Pentecost to be re-enacted. Such an ingathering into the church, I expect then to occur as

has never yet taken place. Christian Israel and the Christian Gentiles will then be one. Their united energies will be turned against sin; and the result will be that their victories for Christ will have no parallel. . . The world will then be ripe for the coming of Christ; and at his coming the holy dead will be raised, the righteous living will be changed, and the millenium will have set in.

It seems to me that contemporary conditions are more favorable to the former presentation (that of Milligan) than to the latter. Is the stage now being set for the coalition of the Beast, the Dragon, and the False Prophet?

CONCLUSION: In the foregoing Lessons 50 and 51, I have presented the theory, held by the great majority of "evangelicals," of the sequence of events that will usher in the Second Coming and the end of the present Dispensation. I should like to state here that I myself, am not committed dogmatically to any particular form of millenialism. I feel that it is an unwise and unjustifiable method of Scripture interpretation to appear in the role of "a prophet on prophecy." I prefer to let the Lord take care of all these matters — I have never yet presumed to transact His business for Him. Any theory of the **sequence** of "final things" must be to some extent speculative and hence cannot be made a test of fellowship in a church of the New Testament order.

As far as my own views are concerned, I must say that I find no evidence in Scripture to support the notion of a general or world-wide acceptance of the Gospel, by either Gentiles or Jews, in the last days of the present Dispensation. On the contrary, the evidence is explicit that these last days will be characterized by a world-wide spread of wickedness, lawlessness, violence, and especially human preoccupation with secular interests, a condition generally paralleling the state of affairs that prevailed in the days before the Flood (Gen. 6:5-13; Matt. 24:29-44; Luke 17: 27-32, 18:8, 21:25-28; 1 Tim. 4:1-5; 2 Tim. 3:1-9; 2 Pet. 3:1-7, etc.). Again, I find no evidence in Scripture and certainly little in contemporary world affairs to warrant the notion of a general turning of the Jews to full accep- tance of the facts of the Gospel of Christ. I am convinced that proof of the Messiahship of Jesus will have to be far more convincing — probably nothing short of the Lord's own appearance at Harmageddon — to convince the Jewish nation as a whole, than is offered simply by the Gospel proclamation. In the third place, the doctrine of the "first resurrection" accords, in my humble opinion, with the apos- tolic description of the ultimate translation of the Church (1 Thess. 4:13-18) than with any other theory of "final things" that has as yet been presented by Biblical commen- tators. That is to say, that as the old Jewish Dispensation terminated with the ascent of the Son to the Father, so the present Christian Dispensation will terminate with the as- cent of the Spirit and the Bride. For this is, in fact, the Dispensation of the Holy Spirit.

However, let it be stated emphatically that there are cer- tain matters in connection with the Great Consummation that are not matters of opinion. Among these are (1) the fact that the Lord Jesus is coming again, (2) that His ap- pearing will be both personal and visible (Acts 1:6-11, Luke 21:27); (3) that His Second Coming definitely will be connected with the Last Judgment and the Consumma- tion of all things (Acts 17:30-31; Acts 3:20-21; Phil. 2:5- 11; 1 Cor. 15:20-28, etc.). The first time He came as the suffering Lamb of God to make atonement for the sins of mankind (John 1:36, 1 Cor. 5:7, 1 Pet. 1:19, Isa. 53:7,

Rev. 13:8, etc.); the second time He will come as the reigning Judge to execute the final destiny of both nations and individuals (Matt. 25:31-46). Then indeed mortality itself will be swallowed up of life — even death itself shall die (2 Cor. 5:1-5), and the saints will appear in the Judgment clothed in "glory and honor and incorruption" (Rom. 2:7), ready to enter upon the inheritance prepared for them from the foundation of the world (Acts 20:32, Col. 1:12, Heb. 9:15, 1 Pet. 1:4, ettc.). Then indeed will Satan and his wicked cohorts, of both angels and men, be segregated in hell for ever (Rev. 20:11-15, 21:8, 22:15).

SPECIAL STUDY: ON THE BOOK OF REVELATION

Revelation of the Risen Christ—Not of John.   Apocalypse—An unveiling.   Signified—Communicated by signs or Symbols.

INTRODUCTION Inscription, 1:1-3.   Prologue, 1:4-8

1:3—"Time is at hand"
1:1—"Things which must shortly come to pass"
4:1—"Things which must come to pass hereafter"

Preterist)
Continuous)
or Historical) Views
Futurist)

A.D. 96—PART I	A.D. 96—PART II	A.D. 96—PART III
Vision of the Seven Candlesticks Ch. 1:9-20 Seven Letters: Chs. 1-3	The Kingdom Vision of a Door Opened in Heaven; the Book with Seven Seals Chs. 4 & 5, Chs. 4:1—11:18	The Church Vision of the Open Temple of God in Heaven Chs. 11:19 to the End
The Church at Ephesus Period, 2:17 Post-Apostolic Age	Opening of the First Six Seals 6:1—7:17	The Woman and the Dragon Ch. 12
The Church at Smyrna Period, 2:8-11 Age of Persecution	The Four Horsemen of the Apocalypse 6:1-8	History of the Beasts Ch. 13
The Church at Pergamum Period, 2:12-17, Union of Church-State	The Opening of the Seventh Seal 8:1-2	The Seven Vials of Wrath 15:1-16:21
The Church at Thyatira Period, 2:18-29 Period of Apostasy	The Sounding of the Seven Trumpets 8:3—11:19	The Mother of Harlots an Abomination of the Earth Ch. 17
The Church at Sardis Period, 3:1-6 Reformation Age	The Angel with the Open Book Ch. 10	Fall of Babylon the Great Ch. 18
The Church at Philadelphia Period, 3:7-13 Restoration Age	The Measurement of the Temple 11:1-14	Zion's Glad Morning Ch. 19:1—20:6
The Church at Laodicea Period, 3:14-22, Period of Lukewarmness	Christ Comes, 11:15-18	Christ Comes 19:11—20:5
Christ Comes 3:20		

Closing Prayer— Conclusion 20:7—22:5
"Come, Lord Jesus!"   Epilogue, 22:6-20

The accompanying diagram of the content of the New Testament book of Revelation follows in part the presentation that appeared in a book by H. C. Williams, a Christian preacher of a century ago. Unfortunately, this book, entitled **The Revelation of Jesus Christ**, first published in 1917, is now out of print. I consider it one of the sanest treatments of the Apocalypse that has ever been published (exclusive, of course, of the time-setting sections in it).

Much as I dislike the overworked word, "interpretation," with reference to the Bible, still and all this book of Revelation is a book which must be interpreted, and interpreted in terms of prophetic symbolism. The content, a series of visions vouchsafed the Apostle John, while the latter was an exile on the barren Aegean island of Patmos, is explicitly said to have been "sign-ified" to the Apostle (1:1). This means, of course, that the Unveiling was couched in symbols. John himself introduces the record of the series of visions with the statement "I was in the Spirit on the Lord's Day" (1:10). The book is generally supposed to have been written toward the end of the first century of our era. (Incidentally, there is a growing conviction among archaeologists in our day that all the books of the New Testament canon were in existence by the seventies or eighties of this first century.)

Three interpretations of the book of Revelation have been suggested by different scholars, namely, (1) the **preteristic,** according to which the events (described by symbols) were fulfilled prior to, and ending with, the destruction of Jerusalem, A.D. 70; (2) the **continuous** or **historical,** according to which the book is a record of the trials and triumphs of Christianity throughout the present or Christian Dispensation; and (3) the **futuristic,** according to which the events recorded will have their actualization in connection with the Second Coming of Christ and the end of the present

Dispensation. For obvious reasons it is the historical view which is accepted and presented here.

Based on the evident fact that Biblical prophecy runs in parallels, it seems clear that we have in the Apocalypse three streams of prophetic utterance presenting the same general history, but from three different points of view as follows: (1) Part One (chs. 1:9 ، 3:22): here we have in the seven letters addressed to the seven churches a kind of prophetic survey of the moral and spiritual changes that were to occur within the visible church; (2) Part Two (chs. 4:1 ، 11:18): in this section we have the record of the Messiah's Kingdom (Reign), of the conflicts between earthly governments and the divine government, until "the kingdom of the world is become **the kingdom** of our Lord and his Christ" (11:18); (3) Part Three (chs. 11:19 ، 22: 5): here we find portrayed the struggles to take place between the true Church, the Bride of the Redeemer, and Satan, the Adversary (working through heresy and apostasy), continuing until the Church, the New Jerusalem, triumphs as the Lamb's wife, and Satan and his rebel hosts are cast into the lake of fire (forever segregated in hell, the penitentiary of the moral universe). (Cf. Eph. 6:12, Luke 10:18, 2 Cor. 4:4, 2 Pet. 2:4, Jude 6.) Each of these Parts is introduced by a distinct vision: Part One, by the Vision of the Seven Golden Candlesticks; Part Two, by the Vision of the Door Opened in Heaven; Part Three, by the Vision of the Open Temple of God in Heaven. Moreover, each Part comes to an end with the announcement of the Second Coming of Christ. In its very symbolism, the entire book is a work of exquisite literary beauty: indeed it is unrivaled in its imagery by anything in either secular or sacred literature.

For all who might be interested, the following sequence of sermon subjects covering the content of the book of Revelation is suggested:

(1) "The Things to Come" (Introductory).

(2) "The Seven Churches of Asia" (Are we now living in the Laodicean Period, the age of lukewarmness and irreligiousness? Is this truly the age of "goodnatured accomodation" to anything that anyone believes? The age of what has rightly been called "convictionless religiosity"?)

(3) "Heaven Through an Open Door" (The Great White Throne and the Lion of the Tribe of Judah)

(4) "The Opening of the Seven Seals" (The Four Horsemen of the Apocalypse and the Sealing of God's Servants)

(5) "The Sounding of the Trumpets" (The Three Winds —The Angels of Woe—the Barbarian Invasions—The Rise of the Papacy and of Mohammedanism)

(6) "The Angel with the Open Book" (Martin Luther and the Reformation)

(7) "The Measurement of the Temple" (The Restoration of Primitive Christianity, its Laws, its Ordinances, and its Fruits)

(8) "The Woman and the Dragon" (The Great Falling Away and the Rise of the Medieval Semipaganized Church)

(9) "The Wild Beasts of the Apocalypse" (The Roman Empire — Constantine and the "Christian" Roman Empire —The Papacy)

(10) "The Mother of Harlots and the Abomination of the Earth" (The Dark Ages — the Rise and Decline of Papal Dominion)

(11) "The Fall of Babylon the Great" (The Image of the Beast—the Union of Church and State—the Rise of Antichrist—Atheistic Leninism—the Zionist Movement and Establishment of the State of Israeli)

What meaneth these things? Are we now witnessing the gradual development of the coalition of the Beast (atheistic totalitarian civil power, misnamed "Communism"), and the Dragon (Oriental paganism), and the False Prophet (Mohammedanism) for the purpose of driving the Jews from Palestine? Will freedom-loving powers of the earth, whether nominally or actually Christian, both Catholic and Protestant, unite in a common defense against this coalition, against the powers that would destroy Christianity (and monotheism) by force? Is this going to be AR-MAGEDDON? Is God's D-Day close upon us?

(12) "Zion's Glad Morning" (The Great Judgment Day —the New Heavens and New Earth. "Come, Lord Jesus!")

(13) "The City of God" (The Tabernacle of God is with Men—The City Foursquare—the Great Consummation)

The foregoing subjects may also be used as topics for study by Bible classes. For additional information, see The Campbell-Purcell Debate, and The History of Apostasies (by Rowe, Hudson, et al). These books may be purchased from DeHoff Publications, Murfreesboro, Tennessee, or from the Old Paths Book Club, Rosemead, California.

SPECIAL STUDY: ON THE ALLEGED
"PRIMACY OF PETER

The entire Roman Catholic system (hierarchy and theology) is based on one claim, and one only, namely, that Peter was the first occupant of the Roman bishopric, and hence that all subsequent occupants of this office were, and are, the divinely authorized successors to the Apostle, clothed with the special authority which, it is held, was vested in him by the Head of the Church Himself, Christ Jesus. The scripture cited for this alleged divine authorization is Matthew 16:13-20. Here we read that, following Peter's voicing of the Good Confession, "Thou art the Christ, the Son of the living God" (v. 16), Jesus said to him, "Blessed art thou, Simon Bar-Jonah: for flesh and blood hath not revealed it unto thee, but my Father who is in heaven. And I also say unto thee, that thou art Peter, and upon this rock I will build my church; and the gates of Hades shall not prevail against it. I will give unto thee the keys of the kingdom of heaven; and whatsoever thou shalt bind on earth shall be bound in heaven; and whatsoever thou shalt loose on earth shall be loosed in heaven" (vv. 17-19). In the Greek text, in the words, "Thou art Peter," the masculine gender (**Petros**) is used, whereas in the phrase that follows, "upon this rock," the feminine form (**petra**) is used. Obviously, since the feminine gender could hardly refer to Peter himself, it must refer to something else, which surely could be nothing other than the **truth** just voiced by the Apostle, the fundamental truth of Christianity, the truth that "Jesus is the Christ, the Son of the living God." In a word, Christ's Church was to be built on the rock of the revealed truth of the Messiahship of Jesus. And the "keys" mentioned by Jesus referred not to Peter's faith, but to the privilege promised him as a reward for it, the "keys" themselves being the terms of admission to the privileges of the New Covenant, that is, to membership in the Church of Christ or citizenship in the Kingdom of Heaven.

The following New Testament facts are sufficient to negate completely any claim that might be made for Peter's primacy or for the absurd notion that Peter himself was the rock on which Christ founded His Church: (1) The promise of "binding and loosing," a well-known Hebraism (implying of course the use of the "keys"), as made to Peter, Matt. 16:19, was repeated later, substantially in the same terms, to the entire Eleven (John 20:21-23). As stated above, the promise to Peter recorded in Matt. 16:19 indicated simply that to him was given the **privilege** of opening the door of the Church (stating the terms of pardon under the New Covenant) to both Jews and Gentiles (as related in the second and tenth chapters of Acts respectively); certainly, however, it did not indicate any special delegation of authority to Peter alone. (2) That the Apostles were of equal rank is further indicated by the language of Jesus in Matt. 19:28, in Luke 22:29-30, in the fourteenth, fifteenth and sixteenth chapters of John, and in Acts 1:1-8. (Cf. also Acts 1:26 and 2:1-4, 2:43, 10:39-42). In all these instances the divine promises are represented as having been addressed to the entire apostolic group, or their fulfillment is pictured as having been enjoyed by the entire apostolic group. (3) The Cornerstone of the spiritual temple of God, the Church of Christ, we are told expressly, is the risen Christ Himself, and the true foundation of this divine Temple is that of the apostolic and prophetic revelation of the Word of truth (Ps. 118:22-24; Acts 4:10-12; Eph. 2:19-22; 1 Pet. 1:10-12). (4) The promise of the advent of the Holy Spirit to guide them into all the truth was made to all the Apostles, and the Holy Spirit was conferred upon all of them alike (John 14:16-17, 14:26, 15:26-27; John 16:7-15; Luke 24:45-49; Acts 1:1-8, 2:1-4, etc.). Paul tells us that he received his knowledge of the Word "through revelation of Jesus Christ" (Gal. 1:12), that is, special revelation to him, as "to the child untimely born," to qualify him to be in a special sense the Apostle to the Gentile world (Acts 26:16-17, 1 Cor. 15:8). (5) There is no evidence from the Gospel narratives that any special revelations were made to Peter that were not made to the other Apostles, with the single exception of the visions on the housetop at Joppa designed to overcome his prejudice against preaching to Gentiles (Acts 10:9-48, 11:1-18, 15:6-11); the evidence is, in fact, to the contrary, namely, that Jesus Himself taught the equality of all the Apostles (Luke 22:24-30, John 13:12-20). (6) In filling the vacancy caused by the fall of Judas from the apostleship, Peter did not arrogate unto himself the authority to appoint Judas' successor; rather, at his own suggestion, the appointment was made by a vote of the entire assembly (Acts 1:15-26). (7) The same demo-cratic method was employed in the choice of "deacons" in the Jerusalem congregation (Acts 6:1-6): indeed it is most significant that the Apostles did not take it upon themselves to appoint these seven men but referred the mat-ter to the entire congregation for a congregational selection. (8) James, not Peter, presided over the first council of Apostles and elders at Jerusalem about A.D. 48. Indeed, it seems that the entire Jerusalem congregation consented to the decrees which were formulated and sent out to the outlying local churches (Acts 15:4-22). (9) Peter himself received a commission (together with John) to go down from Jerusalem to Samaria to qualify the newly-made Sa-maritan converts with the evidential gifts of the Holy Spirit: this he did at the decision and direction of the entire apostolic group (Acts 8:14). (10) Peter himself was taken to task by his Jewish brethren for preaching the Gospel to the Gentiles (in the persons of Cornelius and the mem-bers of his household), and was called on the carpet to make explanations (Acts 11:1-18). (11) Peter was rebuked by Paul, on one occasion at least (Gal. 2:11-21): as someone has facetiously remarked, in this instance the "pope" was rebuked by one of his "cardinals." (12) Peter himself made no claim to primacy among the Apostles or to any special authority over them. He modestly speaks of himself as being only "a fellow-elder, and a witness of the sufferings of Christ" (1 Pet. 5:1; cf. Acts 10:39-41). Surely all this evidence is sufficient to show conclusively that the dogmas of Petrine primacy and of "apostolic succession" in general are figments of the ecclesiastical imagination, and perhaps I should add, "working tools," so to speak, of clerical ambition. And clerical ambition has been the curse of the Church from the time of the Apostles themselves (Cf. 2 Thess. 2:7).

To summarize: Authority is of two kinds, namely, **primary** and **delegated.** The primary Authority in Christianity is, of course, God Himself: He is Perfect Wisdom, Perfect Justice, and Perfect Love (that is to say, He is Wholeness or Holiness). However, the God and Father of our Lord Jesus Christ has seldom chosen to govern men by the exercise of His primary authority. That would be equivalent —would it not?—to government by coercion, that is to say, government by what is commonly designated "miracle." Rather, God has chosen to exercise His authority through His Word as revealed and executed by faithful men: in the Patriarchal and Jewish Dispensations, through the patriarchs, the "judges," the kings, and the prophets, and in the present Christian Dispensation, through apostles, prophets, evangelists, elders and deacons (Heb. 1:1, 11:1-40; 1 Pet. 1:21; John 1:17; Gal. 3:19; Eph. 4:8-16).

The first delegation of authority in Christianity was from the Father to the Son (1 Cor. 11:3, 15:28; Col. 2:9, 1:19, 1:15; Heb. 1:3; John 1:1-3, 1:14, 1:18; Matt. 3:17, 17:5; 2 Pet. 1:16-18, etc.). While the Son, Christ Jesus, was on earth, He exercised His authority (as Uncrowned

King, so to speak) **personally**, as, for example when He forgave sins and when He pardoned the penitent thief on the cross (Matt. 9:6; Luke 23:43; Mark 2:5, 9; Luke 5:20, 23; Luke 7:48). It was not until after His conquest of death, however, that the risen Lord could make the stupendous claim which He did make in prefacing the Great Commission "All authority hath been given unto me in heaven and on earth" (Matt. 28:18; cf. Phil. 2:9-11; Heb. 1:1-4; 1 Cor. 15:20-28).

Now when the Son returned to the Father, after completing the work which the Father had given Him to do (John 17:1-5), another delegation of divine authority became necessary: this was the delegation of authority from Christ the Son to the Apostles whom He had chosen (Acts 1:1-4). Obviously, in the delegation of this authority from the Father to the Son, no danger of error was involved, because the Son was as divine as the Father. (Cf. John 14:6, 9; John 10:30). But the Apostles were human beings, subject to the frailties of body and mind to which all men are subject; hence there was danger that in this second transfer of authority, error might obtrude itself into the Plan of Salvation as a result of the mishandling by the Apostles, of the revelation which Jesus had vouchsafed them while sojourning with them in the flesh. It became necessary, therefore, to qualify the Apostles with divine power and guidance, to clothe them with infallibility in communicating the Christian revelation to mankind. Hence, we read that at different times, Christ promised them the abiding presence of the Holy Spirit to guide them into all the truth, this endowment to take place upon His leaving them and returning to the Father. This promise was fulfilled, as we all know, on the great Day of Pentecost, when the Holy Spirit descended upon the Apostles in baptismal (overwhelming) measure and they all began to speak "as the Spirit gave them utterance." (See John 20:21-23; Matt.

10:18-20; John 17:17-18; John 14:16-17, 14:26, 15:26-27, 16:7-14; Luke 24:45-49; Acts 1:1-8, 2:1-4, 2:32-33, 10:19, 13:1-3, 15:28, 16:6-10, etc.). The mission of the Comforter (Paraclete) specifically was that of clothing the Apostles with authority and infallibility in their task of completing the record of God's revelation to mankind (1 Pet. 1:3; Jude 3; 2 Tim. 3:16-17).

I am now ready to affirm, without fear of successful con-tradiction, that following the first delegation of authority in Christianity from the Father to the Son, and the second delegation from the Son to the Spirit-guided Apostles, **there was no further delegation of such divine authority. There is not one iota of evidence anywhere in the New Testament that the Apostles ever delegated divine authority to any other man or group of men.** The transfer of divine authori-ty ended with the Apostles: they are still exercising this authority through the instrumentality of the Word. The New Testament is the final Word of truth; divine authority for the guidance of the Church is embodied in it. The Gospel is **the power** of God unto salvation. Hence, we repeat that the dogmas of Petrine primacy and apostolic succession are entirely without Scripture warrant.

Divine authority today is in the apostolic testimony, the Word of truth, the New Testament Scriptures (1 Cor. 2:11-16, 1 Thess. 2:13). The specious claim that it was the Church which determined the Canon, and therefore ultimate authority is in the Church, not in the Scriptures, is absurd. The fact is that the Word was at first proclaimed **orally** by apostles and evangelists; this proclamation had to occur first, because by the acceptance of it and obe-dience to its terms, beginning with the three thousand con-verts on the Day of Pentecost, the Church came into exist-ence. (The incorporation of the Body is described in Acts 2:37-47.) Although the Canon was determined later, the Word was the instrumentality through which the Church was established and by means of which it was extended over the Mediterranean world in the lifetime of the Apostles (Matt. 28:18-20, Acts 1:1-8, 8:4; Rom. 10:6-15). Therefore divine authority is in the apostolic testimony as permanently embodied in the New Testament writings, and not in the hierarchical church and its fallible human councils.

C. C. CRAWFORD

Dr. Crawford is well qualified academically and by experience to write in the area covered by the two volumes of *A Survey Course In Christian Doctrine.* Cecil Clement Crawford holds the degrees of A.B., A.M., Ph.D., L.L.D. His undergraduate work was done in Washington University. His graduate degrees of A.M., and Ph.D. were also received from the Washington University. The honorary degree of LL.D. was conferred upon him by the Southwest Christian Seminary. Dr. Crawford also pursued special studies in medieval philosophy at St. Louis University, St. Louis, Missouri. For the past seven years he has been chairman of the department of Philosophy and Psychology at Texas Western College of the University of Texas system, El Paso, Texas. Dr. Crawford is also a member of Phi Beta Kappa, Beta of Missouri Chapter.

He is the author of several very popular books — among them are:

Sermon Outlines On Acts.

Sermon Outlines On The Restoration Plea.

Sermon Outlines On The Cross of Christ.

Sermon Outlines On First Principles.

The American Faith.

ANCHOR IN HEAVEN

"...by two utterly immutable things, the Word of God and the Oath of God, Who cannot lie, we who are refugees from this dying world might have a source of strength, and might grasp the hope that He holds out to us. This hope we hold is the utterly reliable anchor for our souls, fixed in the very certainty of God Himself in Heaven..."
--Heb. 6:18,19 (Phillips Trs.)